creative

PICKLING

CREATIVE
PICKLING

FROM CLASSIC DILLS
TO GINGER PEARS

50 SWEET, SAVORY,
AND TANGY RECIPES

LARK
BOOKS

A Division of
Sterling Publishing Co., Inc
New York

**Barbara
Ciletti**

JANE LAFERLA
Editor

CHRIS BRYANT
Book and cover design
and production, food styling,
and photostyling

EVAN BRACKEN
Photography

CATHARINE SUTHERLAND
HEATHER SMITH
Editorial assistance

HANNES CHAREN
Production assistance

VAL ANDERSON
Proofreader

Library of Congress Cataloging-in-Publication Data

Ciletti, Barbara J.
    Creative pickling : from classic dills to ginger pears, 50 sweet,
savory, and tangy recipes / Barbara Ciletti.—1st ed.
      p. cm.
    Includes bibliographical references and index.
    ISBN 1-57990-177-8 (hc.)
    1. Pickles. 2. Cookery (Relishes). 3. Canning and preserving. I. Title

  TX805.C55 2000
  641.4'6—dc21
                                                    99-086889
                                                 CIP

10 9 8 7 6 5 4 3 2 1

First Edition

Published by Lark Books, a division of
Sterling Publishing Co., Inc.
387 Park Avenue South
New York, N.Y. 10016

© 2000 by Barbara Ciletti

Distributed in Canada by Sterling Publishing,
c/o Canadian Manda Group, One Atlantic Ave., Suite 105
Toronto, Ontario, Canada M6K 3E7

Distributed in Australia by Capricorn Link (Australia) Pty Ltd.,
P.O. Box 6651, Baulkham Hills, Business Centre, NSW 2153, Australia

If you have questions or comments about this book, please contact:
Lark Books
50 College Street
Asheville, North Carolina 28801
(828) 253-0467

Printed in China by Oceanic Graphic Printing Productions, Ltd.

ISBN 1-57990-177-8

acknowledgments

DEDICATION

*This is for Carmela Ciletti—
mother, teacher, and comrade
in kitchen craft.*

THIS BOOK IS ABOUT PICKLING, to be sure. But it's also about time-honored kitchen crafts and the lessons shared by friends. As this volume evolved from a spark of my imagination to detailed and tactile pages, I learned and received much from neighbors, mentors, and comrades who now share in this achievement. Many thanks to all!

A second opportunity to work with the folks at Lark Books has only broadened my appreciation for my publisher, Carol Taylor. She blends humor with wisdom, and I've had the good fortune to share in both. Of course, the camaraderie, the inspiration, and the sheer fun that comes from food talk all reside here, along with the skill and equanimity of my editor Jane LaFerla. This entire volume waltzes with color as well as practical information because of art director (and resident food wizard) Chris Bryant. And our master of the lens, Evan Bracken, has captured the light and the lure of harvest bounty once again.

Neighbors and family have always been a big part of my kitchen activities, and a few special friends generously offered to "get in a pickle" with me. Cathy Morrison, Maybelle Cage, and Mildred Morrison shared recipes for red flannel pickles, delectable sweets, and vintage kitchen tools. Fellow olive lover Olga Cossi contributed valuable information about brining, as well as succulent samples over the years. The folks at Ralston Antiques in Lyons, Colorado, added knowledge, a treasured kitchen scale, and good humor to the mix. (If you're lucky enough to stop by someday, you'll note that they house an impressive array of kitchen utensils, as well as a stunning Victorian milk glass pickle caster.)

contents

introduction

IT'S TIME

Whenever I see the first asparagus in April, catch the scent of plum tomatoes ripening under the July sun, or taste the first fresh-roasted chilies in August, my instincts deliver the same message year after year. Once the snows of winter subside, I cultivate the earth, and it responds with a splendor of herbs, flowers, and fresh vegetables. When the cucumber patch spawns hundreds of little gherkins, when apricots blush with hues of rose and gold, and tomatoes fatten with juice, I prepare to stock my pantry by continuing the lessons of an ancient kitchen craft. It's time to pickle.

In preparing the information for this volume, I realized that I've been canning and pickling for more than 40 years. The words "it's time" became a part of my vocabulary as I worked side by side with my mother from the time I was six years old. During the morning hours, from June through September, we would walk through the vegetable garden or among the apple trees. We often stood still to gaze at the white and blue grapes festooned along the walls and ceiling of the arbor that led to the chicken coop. I watched as she inspected the produce, always astonished that she knew precisely when to announce the harvest.

Her declaration of readiness danced in the air, issuing a call to action. We began to select and harvest green beans, tomatoes, rhubarb, apples, beets, and more for the pantry. We washed, grated, steamed, heated the vinegar, blended spices, inhaled the scents of clove, lemon, mint, and garlic. We filled sterilized jar after jar and popped them into the canner. The kitchen swelled with the volume of our labors, accompanied by the hush of each jar yawning to a close.

My mother's contagious enthusiasm for pickling, canning, and kitchen craft inspires me to this day. At the age of 83, she still loves to add the spice to beets, slice onions for her pickles, or cook up a batch of apples. I've found that her abundant interest and energy for taking the time to make food for the pantry is shared by many contemporary cooks.

PICKLING TODAY

Regardless of the vast array of foods available commercially, pickling and preserving food for home pantries continues to live as an art and craft. Kitchens in Asia, Europe, and North America abound with cooks who appreciate the ability to capture food at its moment of greatness. While chopping jalapeños for salsa, fermenting apples for cider, or brining olives takes a little extra time, patience, and attention to detail, the rewards are well worth the effort.

If you've never tried pickling, you'll find it's easy, fast, fun, and economical—easy because processing involves a simple hot-water bath, fast because recipes are made in small batches, fun because you can create delicious recipes to enjoy and give as gifts, and economical because you can stock your pantry with specialty foods at a fraction of the gourmet-shop cost.

HOW TO USE THIS BOOK

Since pickling preserves food for short- and long-term use, the processing section offers tips for safe pickling, including how to select and prepare equipment and work with essential ingredients. Information about processing times, altitude, and kitchen safety will enable you to harvest and store food for good health.

You'll find guidelines for making your own cider vinegar, information about brining dills or olives, hints for the well-preserved lemon, as well as a cache of recipes selected to celebrate pickled food at its best. Sidebars include kitchen lore, pickle history, and the anecdotes that make kitchen craft fun. And since food remains a perennial gift, you'll see a few ways to share your kitchen creations throughout the year.

While this effort is not all inclusive, it does celebrate imagination, and a few of the kitchen craft pleasures that are a result of my own experience and research. And whether you are a novice or a more experienced kitchen crafter, I'd like to share that message conveyed to me so many years ago. It's time. Enjoy!

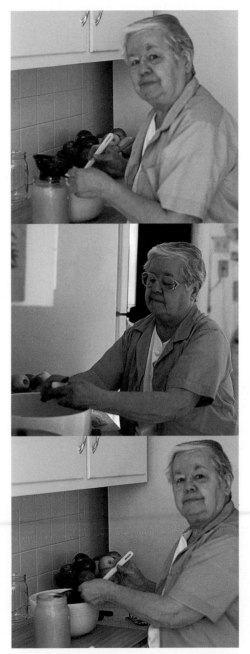

At age 83, my mother, Carmela Ciletti, continues her lifelong love and enthusiasm for pantry crafts.
PHOTOGRAPHS BY ERIC SCHREIBER

pickling through the centuries

a
short
history
of pantry craft

EARLY FOOD PRODUCTION AND PRESERVATION

Recipes for storing food have been a critical influence in food history throughout the world. Today when we pickle, we experience the same sense of well-being that started more than 4,000 years ago when man first began to benefit from, and enjoy, preserved foods. We've learned to save the bounty of the harvest through the cold months and lean times, and we've learned to do it deliciously.

Forty thousand years ago, we can begin tracing the emergence of modern man. Even though we are not quite sure of the average human life span or the social customs of that time, we do know our distant ancestors began to keep or store food long before they cultivated the land. The earliest methods of food preservation involved drying then, later, salting of meats from the hunt.

Approximately 11,000 years ago, man began domesticating plants and animals. The emergence of agriculture became our key to survival, eventually replacing hunting as the sole source of food. The dawn of civilization corresponds to this successful effort at harnessing the wild in a whole new way.

Once people learned they could imitate nature by cultivating edible plants, they took a giant leap toward controlling their food supply. Archaeologists have found that people were eating wild peppers as early as 7000 B.C. and cultivating them after 5200 B.C. Records also tell us that the Chinese had become fairly sophisticated kitchen gardeners as early as 5,000 years ago.

As we learned to grow food, the notion that we could preserve it for future use was not far off. We know that the Egyptians sent their loved ones to the afterworld with onions (the symbol of eternity) on their eyelids, while their tombs housed large jars of wine and other preserved staples for a satisfying afterlife. The ancient Peruvians began preserving peppers as early as 2500 B.C., and ancient Vedic writings from India talk about using and saving onions, garlic, and cucumbers.

FERMENTATION

Methods of survival evolved to include more sophisticated food storage. By approximately 2800 B.C., practices included an understanding of fermentation. The Chinese were not only avidly growing alliums (the flavorful family of onions), they found ways to dry and then later ferment food for long-term use. The great Wall of China may have been built of stone, but it was fashioned by the hands of men fortified with pickled cabbage and garlic.

By approximately 2000 B.C. the Tigris and Euphrates Valley bloomed with grains, figs, and cucumbers that had made their way from India through traders and travelers. Figs were preserved with honey and wine, while cucumbers were consumed in a pickled state. The philosopher Aristotle began to applaud the medicinal advantages offered by pickled cucumbers. Cleopatra is said to have doted on them, believing them to contain the ingredients for everlasting beauty. The Roman Emperor Tiberius made pickles a part of his daily diet. In his *Natural History*, the Roman philosopher Pliny refers to spiced and preserved cucumbers when talking about food and culture.

VINEGAR

Man made good use of the discovery that wine naturally fermented and turned to vinegar. We learned that we could preserve food, eat it, and not get sick (or worse yet, die) when we stored it in an acid solution. Pickling is the process of controlled fermentation, with or without salt, that prevents the growth of microorganisms which accompany food spoilage. The acidic properties of vinegar provided a perfect medium for controlling food fermentation, while making the stored food not only palatable but savory.

cleopatra's delight

The earliest pickles were produced by salting. People discovered that salting food in urns and pots, then burying the vessels, encouraged the production of a juicy, salty liquid—yes, brine! The brine added flavor and acted as a preservative. By Cleopatra's time, brining had become a tradition.

pickled peruvian peppers

The Peruvians provide some of the most ancient records of domestication and preserving of peppers. In fact, peppers were second only to maize in the Peruvian diet. Archaeologists have found dried and crushed peppers, as well as peppers that had been blended with water and other herbs to make sauces and pastes, all of which have been "preserved" for centuries.

The opening of trade routes created a demand for spices, oils, textiles, and preserved food. Through his travels, Marco Polo introduced the European world to pepper and pickles in the 13th century. Christopher Columbus cultivated cucumbers in his experimental garden on Haiti in 1493. Preparing for lengthy sea voyages meant stocking a ship's galley with food that would survive the journey. Pickled food for hungry sailors saved them from starvation and scurvy. Wily merchants learned to ply pickles as trade goods—perhaps making them the first imported "specialty foods."

PICKLING IN AMERICA

American pickling history reflects the story of working the land. Farming, food, and stocking up—filling the pantry and putting food by—thrived in the early days of this country. Our forefathers pickled everything from eggs and walnuts, to cucumbers and artichokes. When good strong cider vinegar couldn't be found, they used white vinegar. Seasoning came from peppercorns, salt, mace, and ginger. Food preservation grew from a home industry to a more commercial American venture when Henry J. Heinz began to bottle pickles in 1870. He began with cucumbers, and went on to offer cauliflower, onions, and a host of vegetables kept in the cider vinegar he produced himself.

From the time of the first settlements, Americans have celebrated their diverse cooking traditions by recreating pickling recipes brought from other lands and cultures. Preparing food was just one way for people to cluster and build community in a new land. To this day, pantry craft remains embedded with sharing our bounty with family and friends. With every home-cured batch of olives, dried bouquet of oregano, or pickled pepper, home cooks keep alive the vibrant recipes of past generations.

Just remember, when you pickle eggs or make a batch of cider vinegar, you are drawing on recipes that began with the Ming Dynasty or in medieval Europe.

PICKLING RENAISSANCE

Today, we enjoy an ongoing and artisanal interest in food that makes us take the time to learn how to produce our own cheese, bake our own bread, and pickle. Even city dwellers sense the primordial urge to preserve the harvest when staring at bushels of tomatoes and corn at the farmers' market.

Though modern transportation brings us produce, meat, and fish from around the world, we still want to produce and preserve our own food as an affordable, healthy, and creative way to eat. While kitchen gardeners and cooks agree that cultivating, then preserving, call for long hours under the sun, then extra time in the kitchen, they also agree on the sense of satisfaction that comes from the scent of herbs and spices "pickling the air" from June through October.

Don't be intimidated by acres of produce. Pickling is food preservation in small dimensions. Eat some now, then pickle a few jars to give away later to friends and family. They'll welcome the sunny taste of summer during the mid-winter doldrums.

PHOTOGRAPH BY CATHARINE SUTHERLAND

arrghhhh! a plague of scurvy upon you

Scurvy plagued sailors on long sea voyages because of the lack of fresh fruits and vegetables containing vitamin C. According to historian Bernabe Cobo, Spanish sailors packed large vats of pickled peppers to bring on board ship, since peppers particularly are such a high source of vitamin C. They then combined the pickled peppers with other foods, such as corn, in order to avoid the dreaded disease.

a discussion for contemporary cooks

GETTING INTO A PICKLE

"How camest thou in such a pickle!" More than 400 years ago, William Shakespeare wrote this line for *The Tempest*. Still considered to be the most brilliant of his comedies, its phraseology reflects the dance between metaphor and the human condition. The "pickle" here illustrates a mood that could only be described as a bit salty and sour, much like the taste of common pickles then and now.

So, why are we so attracted to food in this state? Just compare the taste of standard, home-canned carrots to pickled carrots. The complexity of tastes found in pickles—sometimes sweet, sour, tart, or salty—is a celebration for our senses and embodies the festivity of harvest time from season to season.

Pickling and canning reflect a season of the year that begins in late Spring and can last through early November. Don't be surprised if, once you've put up your first batch, that you find yourself looking for another recipe, and another. You may well get as hooked on the experience as I have. The sparkle of warm cider vinegar, the scent of spiced pears, and the gentle breeze that sends a hint of orange mint through my kitchen window are heaven to my senses.

FILLING THE PANTRY

With a little planning, you can maintain an ongoing supply of basic pantry ingredients that continues the sense of delicious abundance so prevalent during harvest time. Whether you're a novice or a more experienced cook, you'll appreciate the fact that pickling includes, but is never limited to, making pickles—be they cucumbers, onions, or watermelon rind. The primary ingredients of pickling, salt and vinegar, enable you to create a variety of different brines for making everything from catsup to soup bases to homemade sauerkraut.

You'll find that keeping a host of essential ingredients on hand, which you've pickled yourself, can save a trip to the supermarket and enhance your food with many tasty options. A jar of cipollini onions marinating in balsamic vinegar enables you to create a memorable pasta dish or present a quick and elegant appetizer on short notice.

Pickling also encourages you to make a few basic pantry items which may seem beyond your creative scope. For instance, if you own a food processor or a juicer, you can easily make your own cider vinegar (see page 38) and always maintain a fresh batch. While the fermentation process for vinegar, whether cider, wine, or pineapple, requires time, and a dark, warm spot in your kitchen or basement, it doesn't really require much of your energy or attention.

IT'S ALL IN THE TIMING

Pickling is food preparation in small dimensions. You do not need to rearrange your life around it; you can easily regulate your schedule, your workload, and your energy for a delicious yield that can last throughout the year. While you may want to set aside an afternoon or a day to pickle, the process remains a simple one of selecting quality produce, preparing your equipment, and following your creativity.

Whenever I can peaches or make applesauce, I spend several days in the kitchen working with bushels of produce and dozens of large jars. When I pickle, I can use just enough produce to fill one jar, process it for 15 to 20 minutes, and be done with everything in less than an hour.

Some recipes don't even need processing. If you enjoy the preserved lemons found in Moroccan fare or in linguine with clam sauce, you'll be pleased to learn that you can preserve three or four medium lemons in a small jar in less than 30 minutes. The lemons cure in their own juice, along with salt and spices, for several days before they are ready to use in your recipes or to store in the refrigerator where they will stay fresh for weeks.

A HEALTHY HARVEST

Pickling offers healthy eating by capturing food at its peak of flavor and freshness. Like other methods of food preservation, pickling offers good nutrition (when easy on the salt), as well as flavor for up to 12 months after processing. Your food will be higher in essential vitamins (particularly Vitamin C), and free from guar gum, dyes, and chemical preservatives.

Be aware, however, that brining (curing the produce in salt and water) dissipates most, if not all, essential nutrients. Modern-day food historian Waverly Root describes the cucumber as something "neutral" as a vegetable can get. So eat a brined dill pickle for pleasure, but not as a health food!

Fresh produce has become more available in stores throughout the year. In an effort to meet the demands of an ever-expanding world population, much of it has been forced to grow rapidly in unnatural environments. The quality of this produce pales against the vibrancy of vegetables and fruits allowed to ripen on the vine during a full growing season.

When you garden, or even if you purchase fresh produce from the local farmers' market, you're more able to control freshness and thus lose fewer nutrients when preserving. Taste a vine-ripened tomato, then taste a greenhouse-grown specimen; you'll note the vast difference in flavor and texture. In addition, homegrown not only tastes better, it provides more complete nutrients for healthier eating. Even though commercially grown produce is picked fresh before being shipped, many of its vitamins and minerals are lost in the two to three days (or more) that it takes for delivery to the market.

GOOD SENSE

Whenever I go to the market, I see shelves lined with "specialty" foods. There's everything from shitake mushroom with sesame salad dressing to ginger-soy-lime marinade to red raspberry and chipotle vinegar. Many of these products maintain a basic vinegar base, with a blend of fruits, herbs, and spices. These items can also get costly. And while I am continually enticed by the labels, I am also regularly disappointed to find that such a small bottle of raspberry vinegar can carry such a large price.

I must admit that the convenience of the purchase can be quite tempting, but most of the more ethnic or specialty pickled products can be made at a fraction of the commercial price and take less than an hour to assemble in you own kitchen. While pickled eggs, cucumbers, ginger, or homemade brined olives require days or even weeks of steeping time before you can taste the end result, their biggest requirement involves waiting, not working.

Pickles are popular food entries at local fairs. Judges examine the jars for eye appeal, then open them for sampling the flavors. Winners can receive monetary prizes, but most are happy to cherish the blue, red, or white ribbon that denotes a championship pickle.

FAR LEFT: Opened pickles waiting for the taste test

LEFT: The winning pickles

PHOTOGRAPHS BY CATHARINE SUTHERLAND

GETTING TOGETHER

If ethnic food is a culinary universe to explore, then pickling provides the bridge to more than one discovery. Since pickling has been popular for centuries, and enjoyed in nearly every culture, it remains a craft which opens the door to kitchens all over the world.

Experience the food another human consumes, and you'll learn how that person lives, loves, and greets life. Cook with pineapple vinegar and you'll see Mexican food as you never have before. Create a jar of pickled ginger, ferment a batch of sauerkraut, or simply marinate a few figs in vinegar and honey. You'll broaden your journey into the cuisine of other countries, and amplify the array of basic ingredients available to you on a daily basis.

Pickling continues to be an art, as well as an opportunity to build community. Cooks love to explore the world of food while filling their pantries, and most love to share what they make. I can't resist the urge to send a friend home with a jar of jam, a loaf of bread, or maybe a bit of fresh cheese. While I'm sure that this desire comes from childhood influences, I do believe that it's a fairly universal gesture among cooks.

The methods and the meditation that go into cleaning produce, packing jars, juicing fruit for vinegar, or even waiting to hear the "pop" which lets us know that our jars have sealed, get passed along whenever we share from our larder. In a world that sometimes seems to encourage the need for speed, sharing hand-crafted food, especially food that bears thoughtful attention to detail, slows the pace at which we live. We gain and give time to each other. We talk, we laugh, we look at each other. We express a desire for well-being. We are mindful of community. And in the process, we choose how we live today, and how we live tomorrow.

the mount olive pickling company

These early photos from the Mount Olive Pickle Company, Mount Olive, North Carolina, show the commercial dimensions of the pickling process.

PHOTOGRAPHS COURTESY OF THE MOUNT OLIVE PICKLE COMPANY

Filling the capping machine

Bringing in the cucumber harvest

The packing line

pickling basics

more than
a kosher dill

WHENEVER I TALK ABOUT PICKLING I INEVITABLY HEAR THE COMMENT "OH, I *LOVE* PICKLES!" The crock-brined dill, the succulent sweet, and the gregarious pint of bread and butter slices are just the beginning. They are pickles indeed, but they nestle right alongside of thousand-year-old eggs, old-fashioned German sauerkraut, rhubarb angelica, and pineapple salsa.

The "art of the pickle" encompasses food that has been preserved in vinegar or a seasoned brine. The practice itself goes on to include making vinegar and rubbing fruits and vegetables with enough salt to blend with their natural juices to create brine as a secondary product. Feta cheese, for instance, floats in its own brine, which is a combination of the whey and salt used in making curds.

While it shares the basic principles of short- and long-term storage with methods such as canning, drying, making cheese, wine, or sourdough, pickling has its own set of rules. With a few simple tools, fresh produce, and attention to safety, you can enjoy an ancient craft and create a perennial bounty of great food. The first step to success lies in understanding what pickling is and what it does.

THE PROCESS

Pickled food is high-acid food. Simply put, pickling involves the presence of bacteria and yeasts which decompose the sugars found in most foods. This creates lactic acid, as well as acetic acid (vinegar). Elements, particularly salt and vinegar, control the fermentation process, and ensure that pickles have the right balance of friendly bacteria for long-term storage. The taste of this controlled fermentation distinguishes pickled foods from plain, pasteurized canned goods.

If you are a home canner, you know that preserving foods for short- or long-term storage without refrigeration must always involve immersing filled jars in a hot-water bath or processing them in a large pressure canner. This prevents spoilage by heating the food at a sustained temperature to kill bacteria. It also removes air from the jars, creating a vacuum that seals the contents against any airborne contamination.

Due to the high acidity of pickled foods, which naturally inhibits the growth of harmful bacteria, you can process the jarred pickles (including marinades, sauces, and condiments) in a simple covered hot-water bath. This allows short- or long-term storage without refrigeration. Or, for immediate eating, you can opt to simply store them in the refrigerator without processing. You'll find that pickled foods stored in the refrigerator, whether they've been processed or not, will have a longer shelf life than other canned goods; it's the reason catsup can keep for weeks in the refrigerator, while freshly made tomato sauce needs to be eaten within three to five days.

FRESHNESS COUNTS

You may be an avid kitchen gardener, or you may simply enjoy regular visits to the local produce stand. In either case, the first lesson in any form of food preservation lies in selecting the best and freshest ingredients available. Acute attention to pickling instructions, or even the most exotic recipe, won't produce an end result worth keeping when using inferior produce.

Remember, fruits and vegetables begin to decompose once they've been cut, plucked, or picked. Like all living things, they begin to die when separated from their nutrient source. Decomposition, if not stopped early by timely preservation, is a chemical change that can adversely affect the taste of even the most highly spiced pickle recipe.

The ideal standard for pickling or canning involves processing within 24 hours after harvest. Whenever I preserve from the garden, I harvest fruit or vegetables in the cool, early morning hours and pickle that same day. Even if you purchase your produce, make sure that no more than a day or two passes before you get started. The local supermarket can offer usable vegetables and fruits, but check the dates on labels, or ask your greengrocer for information about the source of stock.

Selecting Produce

Some fruits and vegetables are better for pickling than others. Lettuce, for instance, is best consumed fresh. Certain varieties of fruits, or peppers, onions, and cucumbers have been cultivated specifically for canning and pickling. If you are a gardener, seed catalogs or seed packets will make note of these varieties. If you are purchasing produce at a farmers' market, vendors should be able to help you select the best varieties available for the recipes you plan to make.

You can also select or grow young or "baby" specimens for making the perfect pickles. Gherkins (which are really baby watermelons), junior patty pan squash, and immature yellow or red tomatoes, are examples of produce that can be harvested and pickled at varying stages of development.

When picking or selecting fruits and vegetables, always look for plump, firm specimens that are smooth to the touch. Inspect closely for mold, hollow spots, and uneven skin texture. Look for surface scratches, bruises, swelling, or unnatural knobs. All of the above imply unwanted bacteria, enzymes, or the

Once man discovered the connection between growing food and commerce, weekly produce markets became culinary as well as social institutions around the world. This photo was taken at a local farmers' market, an extravaganza of fresh produce. PHOTOGRAPH BY CATHARINE SUTHERLAND

Select the most beautiful produce that you can find. You want to capture the moment of greatness, the peak of perfection.

Selecting produce that is plump and firm to the touch is a good indication of its quality. Then handle your selections gently when washing and rinsing them in preparation for processing or brining.

presence of insects not visible to the naked eye. Also, check the weather forecast and avoid produce that has been harvested after a heavy rain; it will inevitably be water-logged, and not crisp enough to withstand processing.

Search for produce that is free from wax, harmful chemicals, and color treatments. After all, the whole purpose behind the process lies in preserving fresh, untainted, and healthy food. Look for fruits and vegetables that are fairly uniform in size, avoiding any over-grown specimens. Uniformity of size ensures that your recipe will process or pickle evenly, and you'll enjoy a consistent end product.

As you peruse the garden or market, be sure to avoid choosing overripe produce for pickling. While it's fine for ready consumption, it usually contains excess water, which implies a breakdown of the plant sugars. Whether you decide to process your pickled food or just allow it to ferment, you don't want it to fall apart during processing or in the jar on the shelf.

Handling Produce

Regardless of the season or the method of preservation, always handle produce gently. Under cool running water, use your hands or a soft vegetable brush to wash away any soil. Avoid vigorous scrubbing that can create bruises. Be sure to rinse the produce thoroughly. As you wash, be mindful of removing all blossom ends from cucumbers, pickling peppers, and small squash; they are a source of enzymes that encourage spoilage. Pat the washed and rinsed produce dry with a soft, lint-free towel. As you do so, make a final inspection for spots or insect visitors which may have escaped the first round of examination.

You should try to pickle produce immediately after washing and drying. Extended exposure to air can encourage unwanted organisms that will eventually spoil your pickle recipes. If you can't start processing right away, place your food in plastic bags, and refrigerate it until you're ready. Just remember that pickling success may be limited the longer your food sits after being harvested.

PICKLING INGREDIENTS AND PRINCIPLES

Salt and vinegar are the primary ingredients for making pickles. Pickled food falls into two categories: food that ferments in salt or brine, and food that's preserved fresh in vinegar. Sauerkraut, for example, is cabbage that ferments with salt as it sits in a crock. Brined pickles, also known as cured pickles, are cucumbers that ferment in a salt and water solution (brine) in a crock. Lactic acid, which forms in the presence of the salt, brings about the desired fermentation. In order to enhance flavor and crispness, vinegar, spices, and grape or cherry leaves can be added to the salt brine.

Although a pickle wouldn't be a pickle without salt, you can make pickles successfully without the process of brining. Since brined or cured pickles are so high in sodium, pickling with vinegar provides a tasty alternative for those of us who need to watch salt intake. These recipes usually call for an overnight soak (or sometimes none at all) in salt water. Then you process the pickles in a strong, hot solution of vinegar. You may want to check low-salt cookbooks and canning guides for recipes that will suit your dietary needs before getting started. Then select the method and ingredients which most appeal to you.

The balance between salt and vinegar not only affects long-term preservation, it affects the crunch as well as the flavor of your finished pickled product. While both ingredients thwart the growth of unwanted microorganisms, an excess of either one creates an unpalatable pickle. Too much vinegar can slow down, or even halt, the fermentation process, while too much salt creates an overly brined product, which has been completely stripped of any nutrition.

Ingredients

After selecting the freshest, most beautiful produce available, you'll also want the best ingredients for complementing the process. The following items will enhance the flavor of your pickles and ensure the success of your endeavors.

Pickling keeps the freshness and flavor of food through the process of controlled fermentation. A few ingredients such as quality noniodized salt, cider or white vinegar, and pickling lime capture the freshness of the harvest for up to 12 months. Herbs, spices, garlic, peppers and onions add delightful flavor dimensions to vegetables and fruit.

CANNING SALT contains no iodine, and remains free of noncaking agents. Never use iodized salt, since iodine darkens food during preservation. Any additives to salt, including noncaking elements, can create a chemical reaction which results in a cloudy end product. Canning salt is granulated, but a bit coarser than iodized table salt. It can be purchased in five pound bags, and remains available all year long.

Once you begin to shop, you'll find a number of additional salt varieties which safely preserve produce. Kosher salt is also pure and iodine free. For smaller batches of pickled goods, or for the sake of experimentation, you can also try coarse as well as fine sea salt. Just be sure to read the label for processing information. Remember that unlike finer varieties, coarse salt doesn't settle into a measuring cup. You'll need to weigh it on a kitchen scale for accuracy.

Any salt that looks dubiously off-white indicates more than salt in the contents; do not use it for pickling. The greener varieties of sea salt contain seaweed, which can lead to spoilage of canned goods. Almost without saying, avoid any salt, such as rock salt, which isn't intended for human consumption.

VINEGAR is a high-acid food, yet not all varieties are meant for pickling. Look for vinegar that indicates a five to six percent acidity level. While homemade vinegar makes for delicious cooking, its acidity can vary. I do not use it for pickling. If you make a batch of vinegar and want to try it with your favorite pickle recipe, be sure to check the pH level beforehand. You can purchase litmus paper or a wine acid titration kit from a number of canning supply or beverage-brewing catalogs (see Special Thanks on page 126).

Commercially produced American vinegar is standardized and offers reliable results. Seven is the middle of the pH scale, representing the equal balance of acid and alkaline in food. Numbers higher than seven on the scale refer to elements that are higher in alkaline. To be on the safe side, use vinegars that read 5 or lower on the pH scales, such as cider and white distilled vinegar. Following is further information about the vinegars most commonly used in pickling.

APPLE CIDER VINEGAR is much more robust, and will change the flavor and the color of your pickled produce. It works well with cucumbers and zucchini, which aren't adversely affected by the slightly darker tones they adopt. This vinegar is readily available in supermarkets, and maintains a standard five percent acidity, which is perfect for pickling.

BALSAMIC VINEGAR is often compared to nectar. Once you taste it you will know why. This vinegar isn't the industrial canning variety, and since it is typically made in Italy, it fetches a high price in American markets. It's a thick, somewhat resin-like fluid that graces fresh produce with a royal touch. While I don't use it when processing foods, I find that it offers a tangy yet slightly caramel flavor to small sweet onions or fresh strawberries. Try a little for marinades, sauces, or short-term refrigerator pickles. The unmistakably creamy texture of this acetic (six percent and sometimes higher, depending on age) brew will keep you looking for more—you'll treasure the flavor, regardless of what you pay.

DISTILLED VINEGAR doesn't change the color of food, but remains a fairly tasteless liquid. I use it for sweeter fruits such as cherries or blueberries, because it enhances, but does not transform, the flavor of the fruit.

RICE WINE VINEGAR (also called mirin) can be found in Asian markets, health food stores, and most supermarkets. It is vinegar made from fermented rice, which forms the basis of sake and other alcoholic beverages. While it's not meant to make the perfect dill, it provides a valuable flavor dimension to teriyaki sauce and other Eastern specialties. It's lower in acidity and is not suitable for foods you pickle for long-term pantry use. Yet it will yield a shelf life of four to six weeks when used for short-term storage in the refrigerator.

WINE VINEGAR, both red and white, is most frequently used to adorn fresh greens and cooked dishes, but they will add a distinctive splash and sparkle to preserved produce. White wine vinegar adds flavor without changing the color. Red wine vinegar enhances flavor and will create a slightly darker pickle. Red, white, and rice wine vinegar offer varying acetic solutions. The pH of rice wine vinegar frequently measures in at less than five percent, and forms a flavorful base for sauce, but needs an additional boost from another vinegar if you're intending to use it for pickling. I combine rice wine vinegar with white wine or even white distilled vinegar when I prepare pickled food for processing.

Firming Agents and Aromatics

Firming agents, such as pickling lime, help fermented pickles retain their crispy crunch. A number of aromatics offer flavor and dimension to pickled food. Your supermarket shelf probably remains well-stocked with both during picking season.

Pickling lime (more technically, calcium hydroxide) is an alkaline element that blends with pectin. Its alkaline base helps to control the fermentation process. Without a firming agent, fermentation can produce flabby, soft pickles. The use of lime ensures that snap-on-first-bite crunch that contributes to the tactile delight of eating pickles.

Many modern pickling methods have dispensed with the use of lime, or another firming agent called alum (potassium aluminum sulfate). Alum, in particular, can cause a certain amount of digestive distress. Although some will argue that pickling lime and alum aren't necessary, I think they do enhance a pickle's crispness—it's all a matter of taste.

Aromatics, otherwise known as herbs and spices, are perhaps my favorite pickling ingredients. I add some herb, spice, or root to just about everything I pickle. Some of the most common ones used in pickling are angelica, dill, and garlic.

Angelica, with its sweet, anise undertones, enhances the flavor of rhubarb in pie as well as in pickles. Touted for its culinary as well as medicinal uses in the Middle Ages, this popular herb is still used for adding a slight licorice flavor to candy. Then there's dill, which is so easy to cultivate and use liberally—whether fresh or dried. A dill simply wouldn't be a dill without it. Garlic, of course, remains the queen of the garden, and the reigning monarch in cuisines throughout North America, Asia, and Europe.

The combinations of herbs and spices will determine the taste of your pickles. You can be as creative as you dare. For heat and a twist of spice, try allspice, mace, peppercorns, garlic, hot onions, horseradish, or ginger. For a mellow, slightly sweeter result, try caraway, lemon verbena, thyme, marjoram, angelica, or celery seed. A culinary herb and spice chart, or source book, can provide additional information about complementing food with the right herbs and spices.

A CACHE OF SPICE

Spice blends have long coaxed otherwise hidden flavors from cucumbers, zucchini, and beets. Add this spice blend to a jar of pickles to evoke the autumnal flavor of frost on the pumpkin.

INGREDIENTS

1 cinnamon stick, broken into 1/2-inch (1.3 cm) pieces

3 bay leaves, dried and broken

1 teaspoon crushed green peppercorns

1 teaspoon whole cloves

2 teaspoons coriander

1/2 teaspoon juniper berries

1/2 teaspoon nutmeg

1 tablespoon whole dill seeds

METHOD

Place the spices in a small jar, cap it, and shake to blend. Keep for pantry use, or create small sachets as gifts for your favorite cook.

When flavoring your recipes, place the spices in a spice bag or tea ball for cooking. Make your own spice bag from a small square of unbleached muslin or cheesecloth. Place the spices in the middle of the fabric, then tie up the ends with kitchen twine to form a small bag. Consider making these "flavor sachets" as gifts for your favorite cooks.

HOW TO PICKLE

Once you know how to select produce and how to handle it, have explored the world of vinegar, essential ingredients, and the fun of aromatics, you are ready for the next step—how to pickle. Many of the guidelines that apply to canning also apply to pickling. The following information offers basic instructions and includes the critical canning standards. You will learn about equipment, packing the jars, processing in a hot-water bath, and the brining process.

Equipment

Reliable equipment, like quality produce, enables consistent results when you're working with recipes that require processing. With the exception of a boiling-water-bath canner, or a produce scale, your kitchen probably contains most of the equipment listed here:

- A boiling-water-bath canner
- An accurate food thermometer
- Tongs
- A flat knife or commercial bubble freer
- A wide-mouth fruit funnel
- Measuring cups and spoons
- A colander or strainer
- Clamps for lifting jars out of boiling water
- Canning jars—quarts (1 L), pints (.5 L), and half-pints (.25 L)
- Rims with lids, or rubber gaskets
- Long-handled spoons
- Scales (optional), used for recipes requiring measurement by weight
- Towels

Quality equipment assures pickling success. Items such as a boiling-water-bath canner, standardized canning jars with reliable seals, a wide-mouth funnel, and tongs for handling the hot jars will help you get a good start on the process.

A kitchen scale ensures accurate measurement for ingredients. Remember to use nonreactive containers and utensils when pickling to avoid any contamination to high-acid foods.

When pickling, use ceramic, stone, or glass jars. Avoid using containers and utensils made from copper, brass, or galvanized metal. These materials usually react to pickling food, causing discoloration of the material and unwelcome color changes to your product.

Use jars specifically made for home canning. They are readily available at general-merchandise and home-supply stores, supermarkets, and from canning suppliers. They come in many sizes and shapes, including some with decorative motifs. Canning jars are specifically made to withstand the high temperatures of processing. They are economical, since they can be used many times over. Do not reuse jars that you've saved from the grocery store, they will not ensure a safe seal and can break during processing—few things are messier than a broken bottle in your canner.

Canning jars come in two styles based on their sealing methods. One is a screw top with separate rim and lid that has a built-in rubber seal. Once the jar is opened and emptied, the lid must be discarded. While you can reuse the jar and rim, you must use a new lid each time you process. The second style utilizes a round rubber seal (gasket) that you place between the jar's rim and top. The rubber seal is held in place with either built-in or separate clamps. When you purchase jars, take time to review the manufacturer's instructions for use.

Sharp knives make your work easier. When shredding large amounts of produce, consider using a shredder (right) to speed up the process. This one comes in handy when making sauerkraut.

botulism

The spore-forming bacteria *clostridium botulinum* can cause botulism. However, properly processing pickles will keep you away from this pesky microorganism. Even though most pickles are considered high-acid foods, pay close attention to the correct procedures of hot-water bath processing. This will sufficiently secure your bounty for long-term storage.

Use standardized canning jars for your pickling. Although they follow quality control standards, always inspect each item before and after sterilizing in preparation for filling. Once you've packed your produce, inspect them again. The jar rim, and the lid should be free from any food particles, water, nicks or scratches. All can interfere with a complete seal.

Altitude Adjustments for Hot (Boiling) Water Processing	
IF YOUR ALTITUDE (IN FEET) IS:	
sea level to 3,000	add 5 minutes to processing time
3,001 to 6,000	add 10 minutes to processing time
over 6,000	add 15 minutes to processing time

Filling the Jars: Hot and Cold Pack

Before use, you should check jar rims for any cracks or chips. Also check the rubber seals for any cracks and cuts. These factors can cause an incomplete seal during processing, and will expose the jar's contents to spoilage. It is always best to sterilize jars, seals, and rims with boiling water before filling. You can immerse them in boiling water, or pour boiling water over them, then allow them to cool before filling.

There are two ways to fill jars, hot pack and cold pack (also known as raw pack). The hot-pack method is used for most vegetables and fruits. Food is pre-cooked or steamed before being put into hot jars and processed in a hot water bath. I prefer this method for cooked salsa, catsup, barbecue sauce, and marinades or teriyaki.

The cold-pack method starts with cold, uncooked food (such as sauerkraut). The food is packed into the jar and covered with just enough hot liquid to cover the surface of the food. The jars are then processed in a covered hot-water bath like any other canned food. Caution: Jars going into the hot-water bath need to be hot regardless of the contents. If you decide to cold pack, be sure the liquid that you pour over your veggies and fruits is hot. Otherwise, your jars will probably break as they heat up during processing.

For both hot and cold pack, leave approximately $\frac{1}{2}$ inch (1.3 m) of head space (head room) between the top of the liquid and rim of the jar to allow room for expansion during processing. Use a flat knife or bubble freer to eliminate any pockets of air that can cause spoilage. Gently move the knife or freer down the side of the jar. You'll see air bubbles rise to the surface and escape.

Note that altitude can be a factor in preserving the freshness and flavor of processed produce. If you plan to pickle with the hot-water bath, be sure to check processing times for your altitude. Your resident state extension service can provide information for reliable results. The chart at the left shows guidelines as recommended by the Ball Corporation.

Some thick-skinnned fruits and vegetables, like the jalapeños shown here, need to be pierced before packing. This allows the brine to completely penetrate the produce for even pickling.

To avoid bruising your produce, always pack it loosely in the jars.

Whether you pack your pickles raw (cold pack) or already cooked (hot pack), the food needs to be immersed in hot liquid in preparation for the hot-water bath. Here, the hot pickling solution is being poured over the cold-pack jalapeños. Remember to leave approximately ½ inch (.3 cm) of head room between the surface of the food and liquid and the top of the jar.

Be sure to use a nonreactive flat utensil such as a slim spatula or commercial bubble freer to slide down the side of the jar and free excess air bubbles.

Bring the water to a boil, then gently lift your pickling jars into the water. Add more hot tap water if necessary to keep all the jars immersed. Cover the canner and allow the water to return to boil before counting your processing time.

Once your pickled goods have been processed, gently lift them out of the hot-water bath and place them on a towel in a quiet, draft-free spot in your kitchen. They should rest for 12 to 24 hours to complete their seal.

Processing in a Hot-Water Bath

Once you fill the jars and cap them, you will process them in a covered, boiling, hot-water bath, which pasteurizes the food to ensure the elimination or death of harmful bacteria. This keeps food free from spoiling for short- or long-term storage without refrigeration (for instance, on your pantry shelves). Whether you cold pack or hot pack, you will need to follow this method.

After you've packed and capped your jars of food, gently lower them into the canner. Add just enough additional boiling water to cover the tops by 1 inch (2.5 cm). You'll notice that the water will slow down its boil. Return the water to a full boil, then cover the canner with its lid, and begin to count the processing time. It is very important to remember that you begin counting the processing time only *after* the water returns to a boil.

During the processing time, lay folded towels on your countertop, table, or other draft-free spot in the kitchen. When the processing time is completed, use the tongs or clamps to remove the jars from the canner. Place the jars, top up, on the towels and allow them to cool for 12 hours. If you are close by when the jars are cooling, you can hear the seal on a rim-and-lid jar "pop" as it cools.

Once the jars are completely cooled, and before storing them, test the seals. To test the seal on a rim-and-lid jar, press the middle of the lid. If it springs to the touch, it is not sealed; if it remains concave, the seal is good. For jars with a separate rubber gasket, apply gentle pressure while trying to lift the lid of the jar. If the top does not open, the seal is good; if it opens, the seal is bad.

If you have jars that did not seal, you can refrigerate the jars for use within five to seven days, or consume the products the same day. However, if you are ever in doubt about the safety of any food which has not sealed properly, it is always best to discard the food. Just follow the simple phrase, "When in doubt, throw it out."

THE BRINING PROCESS

Brined pickles, such as sauerkraut, cucumbers, or other high-acid vegetable blends, have been immersed in a salty solution which may or may not contain vinegar. Some recipes call for salt only, while others call for additional ingredients, such as vinegar, spices, and herbs. Since brining is done at room temperature, salt is critical to control the spoilage caused by microorganisms. At the same time, the salt is the catalyst for fermentation or the development of "friendly" bacteria that creates lactic acid by breaking down the sugars in food. The lactic acid usually creates a scum, so you should check your brine crock daily, and skim the scum from the surface.

Brining really is pretty simple, and you'll enjoy the snap of your first homemade cucumber pickle right out of the crock. However, serve your pickles for pleasure without regard for their nutritional value—the brine solution drains 75 to 100 percent of vitamins B and C out of pickled food. You may want to look for brining recipes that don't require several weeks of immersion, since the finished product stands a better chance of retaining at least some nutritive value. Personally, I prefer the shorter method of brining. I don't want to wait any longer than absolutely necessary for my first pickle!

Crocks and Jars

You can brine pickles in any size crock. While the larger ones hold an ample supply of produce, they are almost impossible to move once you fill them with produce and brine. Unless you plan to share a considerable quantity of pickles, consider going down a size or two. I frequently use a 1-, 2-, or 3-gallon (3.8, 7.6, or 11.5 L) crock for brining dills. My 3-gallon (11.5 L) crock holds approximately 40 medium pickles, which translates to approximately 5 pounds (2.27 kg) of produce.

Once you obtain a crock or two, you'll find that they come in handy for foods other than brined pickles. If you've used them elsewhere, be sure to scald your crocks (and any utensils) before and after brining. You can also ferment a small batch of pickles in either a quart (1 L) or half-gallon (2 L) jar. Just follow the same guidelines for filling them as you would for a larger crock.

Layering fresh cucumbers with grape, dill, or cherry leaves provides a good flow of bacteria and air necessary for the fermentation process.

Always leave the top third of your crock free to allow the fermentation bubbles to rise.

Pour your brine over the pickles and top them with a clean heavy plate. The pickles need to stay immersed. You may want to place a small jar of water on top of the plate if you need extra weight.

After fermentation is complete, lift the pickles out of the brine with tongs. You can pack them directly in jars, or rinse them until the degree of saltiness is to your taste.

Filling the Crock

Plan on filling the crock two-thirds of the way full with the produce and enough brine to totally immerse it. Leaving the top third of the crock free allows enough head room for fermentation; you'll be able to watch the fermentation bubbles rise but not climb up over the top of the crock, down the sides, and onto the floor.

Most recipes will suggest a brine strength for quart (1 L) as well as gallon (3.8 L) containers. However, I've learned that brine strength can be adjusted somewhat to personal taste. A little experimentation will allow you to maintain the concentration, without spoiling your efforts.

Whether you ferment the pickles in a crock or jar, you will need to weight the pickles to keep them immersed in the brine. To do this, place a dish on top of your pickles and brine, and add just enough extra weight on top of the plate to ensure immersion. For extra weight, I use a pint (.5 L) jar filled with water, or a plastic bag filled with water and tied. Whichever weight you use, just be sure that all of the pickles are snugly covered. One protruding potential dill can ruin the whole batch when exposed to the air—and airborne bacteria.

Skimming and Processing

While the development of a certain amount of yeast on the surface of the brine is common for fermented pickles, you will want to check your crock daily and remove the yeast and any scum that may be present. Skimming the scum limits the growth of mold which can cause mushy and dark, rather than bright and crisp, pickles. I use a large shallow spoon or a loosely woven kitchen towel to skim the surface.

Once the pickles have completed their transformation, you will need to store them. Depending on the recipe, some fermented pickles are brined and stored, while others are brined, then processed in a hot-water bath before storage. You may want to experiment with both methods and decide which result yields the perfect pickle for you. Pickles always taste best when consumed within six months.

PROBLEM PICKLES

Not every batch of pickles offers a perfect yield. If you run into less than desired results, you may have interrupted the process for any number of reasons including variables in temperature, the type of salt used, or the acidity of the vinegar. Following are the problems you may encounter and their probable cause for the result.

SOFT, MUSHY PICKLES: All of the pickles may not have been immersed in brine, despite your best efforts. Or, the surface contained too much scum (not enough skimming) and yielded the growth of too much mold.

PUCKERED AND SHRIVELED PICKLES: Too much vinegar or too much salt in the brine will retard fermentation and cause your pickles to wither.

DULL, DARK, OR WASHED-OUT COLOR: You've selected produce that is too mature, used a utensil that contains iron, or used water that is hard with minerals.

SPOILED PICKLES: Generally, the process wasn't done properly. Major causes are using old ingredients, reusing lids, a hot-water bath that wasn't hot enough, or rushing the process.

HOLLOW PICKLES: You may have used produce that lost its freshness. Remember, the time from vine to the canner should take as little time as possible.

seeing red

The world's largest catsup bottle soars above the town of Collinsville, Illinois, located 12 miles northeast of St. Louis, Missouri. The giant bottle, actually a water tower, has its own international fan club, and is listed in the National Register of Historic Places.

The tower was built in 1949 to supply fire protection to the Brooks Foods bottling plant, makers of "Brooks Tangy Old Original Catsup." At the time, Brooks was the town's largest employer. The bottle not only instilled a sense of pride in the community, it provided a unique way for the company to advertise its product.

Though the plant stopped processing catsup in 1962, the building and tower remained as a company warehouse. When the property changed ownership in 1993, the town couldn't think of tearing down the then beloved landmark. Instead, they mounted an effort to restore the bottle to its former glory.

Today, you can purchase T-shirts, hats, and other memorabilia that commemorate this bit of classic roadside architecture.

FOURTEEN SIMPLE STEPS FOR PICKLING SUCCESS

Following these steps will help ensure a perfect and safely processed pickled product.

1 Whether you are canning or pickling food, use soft or distilled water. Minerals, particularly iron, will cause the discoloration.

2 Use half-pint (.25 L) or pint (.5 L) jars for most pickles processed with the hot-water canner. Otherwise, you need to increase the canning time, which can result in overly processed, dull, rather tasteless food.

3 Check jars for cracks along the rim, and check the seal for any cuts or cracks in the rubber. These inconsistencies tend to be the chief cause of improperly sealed food and subsequent spoilage.

4 Sterilize all utensils, especially the jars an lids, before use. This will continue the war on harmful bacteria.

5 Always wipe the rims with a clean, lint-free cloth before and after placing food in the jars. Any particles of food or liquid can interrupt a proper seal and create spoilage. You'll know within 24 hours if your jar has failed to seal into an air-tight state; spoiled food has a distinct odor-and hiss.

6 Loosely pack or ladle your food into hot jars, leaving about ½ inch (1.3 cm) of head room between the food and the top rim. This will leave enough room for expansion when the jar is in the hot-water bath.

7 Use a sterile, flat butter knife or a commercial bubble freer to run down the sides of filled jars. This releases any air bubbles without damaging the food. Cover the jar with the rim and cap, and screw or secure them firmly into place.

8 Fill your canner one-third of the way with water before bringing it to a boil. Place your jars in the canner and add just enough water to immerse them approximately 1 inch (2.5 cm) below the water's surface. Bring the water back to a boil before starting the countdown on the processing time.

9 Be sure to cover the canner with its lid once the jars are in place. Open-bath or kettle processing can be dangerous for everything but jams and jellies. Processing without the lid fails to ensure a constant temperature and adequate pressure for creating a seal. Add boiling water as necessary to keep the jars 1 inch (2.5 cm) below the surface of the water.

10 Remove your processed pickles from the canner and place them top up on a towel in an area of your kitchen which is free from drafts.

11 You may hear your jars "pop" as they cool. The decrease in temperature seals the vacuum created by processing in boiling water. Allow the jars to sit for at least 12 hours before testing the seal. If you are using rim-and-lid jars, press the center of the lid. If it doesn't pop back up, the jar is sealed. If the lid looks concave, or curved down toward the middle, your jar is sealed. If you are using jars with a separate rubber gasket, test the seal of the cooled jars by gently trying to lift the top. If it does not yield to your pressure, it is sealed.

12 Even though the jars may contain hot liquid, don't invert, or turn them upside down in order to seal them; the heat may be inadequate for a good seal.

13 Store your processed pickles in a cool, dark pantry or fruit cellar in order to avoid the fluctuations in temperature which can, at times, cause a breakdown in the texture of your product. Too much heat can also cause the lid to pop, and this will break the seal, rendering spoiled food. The average shelf life for canned or pickled food extends from 6 to 12 months.

14 Generally, canning pickles of any variety simply calls for reliable and standardized canning equipment, attention to safety, and diligence when watching the clock.

vinegar

A BOOK ABOUT PICKLING would be less than complete without a few recipes for homemade vinegar. Vinegar was probably one of the first happy kitchen accidents to occur when soured wine first made its way to the palate. Today we make vinegar from wine, beer or malt, apples, pineapple, and other fruit. This naturally fermented liquid requires a simple procedure and the patience to allow nature to work its magic.

The contemporary uses for vinegar extend far beyond its culinary features. Its value as a hair rinse, stain remover, and window cleaner make it a household staple. Yet, once you've created your very own first batch, you'll prefer to keep it in the kitchen and leave the windows for another remedy.

This section will discuss the process that produces acetic acid, or vinegar, along with a few tips and recipes to make the process enjoyable. While the basic chain of chemical events remains universal, I've included additional information to address the characteristics of the specific varieties. You'll find a recipe for cider vinegar, along with pointers for making wine, pineapple, and berry vinegars.

VINEGAR BASICS

Vinegar undergoes two stages of fermentation as juice first converts to alcohol, then undergoes a second or continued fermentation that produces the solution known as acetic acid (vinegar). Following is a summary of these events.

Cider, fruit, and wine vinegar start from fresh fruit which has been chopped or pulverized, creating the *must*, which is then pressed to extract the juice. For apple cider vinegar, the process starts with crushing and squeezing the produce. Wine vinegar starts with the pressing of the grapes, followed by the making of wine, which is then allowed to turn into vinegar.

Apple must and juice can be produced with a juicer or a food processor. If you use a food processor, you'll need to strain the juice into the crock or jar for fermenting. A juice extractor, which separates the must automatically, does all of the work for you.

The "mother," a leathery scum of bacteria, converts fermented juice or cider to acetic acid. You can make your own by allowing juice to sit for 3 months or more. Or, you can purchase a small quantity to create your first batch of vinegar, then save a portion of the mother for future use.

The extracted juice needs to stand in consistently warm temperatures of 70 to 85°F (21 to 29°C) until a growth of yeast bacteria begins to form on the surface of the liquid. This is the first step of the fermentation process. Raw apple juice ferments to form cider, and grape must ferments for the beginning stages of wine.

During the first stage of fermentation, which converts the liquid to alcohol, your liquid will foam and bubble as the bacteria proliferate. Left to nature, the growth of the wild or airborne yeast will take the liquid through the two stages of fermentation to produce vinegar, but this can take several months. While the result is reliable, you may want to purchase additional yeast to speed up the process. This yeast is available from vinegar- and beverage-making suppliers (see Special Thanks on page 126). Make sure you purchase yeast that is specific to the vinegar you wish to brew. You can find yeast for making cider, malt, and white and red wine vinegar.

Once the liquid has been saturated with yeast bacteria and ceases to foam, the surface will start to develop a rather rubbery-looking scum called the *mother*. The mother, whose presence indicates the beginning of the second step of fermentation, allows the liquid to change from alcohol to acetic acid. This step in the process can take several weeks.

If you would like to accelerate the conversion from alcohol to acetic acid, you may want to use a commercial variety of mother, also available from vinegar- and beverage-making suppliers. In many ways, the mother behaves like other starters such as sourdough, yeast sponge for bread, or cheese-starter culture; you can save a bit of the mother from one batch to start another.

In order for the mother to develop, the juice, cider, or wine needs plenty of circulating air, as well as a still, dark environment. Too much sun or heat will kill bacterial growth, and movement of your container may force the scum to drop to the bottom. When this happens, bacterial growth may be permanently impaired, since the scum (mother) forms from the oxygen that circulates above the surface of the fermenting liquid. Once it flops to the bottom of the container, the bacteria will continue to feed off of the nutrients in the liquid, but can't get enough air for the oxidation to continue; this will bring your vinegar production to an abrupt halt. Don't confuse sediment with the mother. Sediment is a solid residue from the unfiltered liquid; it will inevitably reside at the bottom of wine and raw, unfiltered cider.

As the fermented liquid continues to sit with its mother, the alcohol continues to breathe in the surrounding air to form acetic acid. Vinegar is born. Since the fermentation process continues until forced to stop, vinegar must be strained, or clarified, then pasteurized (heated) to kill bacteria that would spawn ongoing chemical activity. Once vinegar is pasteurized, it's cooled and bottled for future use. If you plan to make more vinegar, you can save the mother culture in a bottle made of brown glass, or any other opaque variety that prevents light and air from encouraging bacterial growth.

When I first began making vinegar, I found the process a bit confusing, because I was looking for two distinct steps in the fermentation process. In actual fact, the formation of alcohol (the first fermentation) naturally leads to the formation of acetic acid (the second fermentation). Adding yeast or a mother to your juice or wine simply accelerates the timing of nature's procedure.

GETTING STARTED

Vinegar can fail if temperatures fluctuate too dramatically and conditions aren't sanitary. Following are a few tips that will help you set the stage for successful vinegar making.

For wine vinegar, always use a quality red, white, or varietal wine, with at least 10 percent alcohol saturation. Vinegar requires a 10 to 15 percent alcohol level for wine to convert to vinegar. This includes rice wine, as well as other alcoholic beverages.

If you plan to make vinegar from apples or other fruit, be sure that the fruit is perfectly ripe, making sure that it is not even a little green or not a little overripe. Too much or too little sugar, depending on the fruit's stage of ripeness, can upset the balance required for fermentation.

For fruit vinegar, such as cider vinegar, use fruit high in sugar and fiber, such as winter and not summer apples. Summer apples don't contain the fructose needed for fermentation. Other fruits such as pineapple, papaya, and grapes are good candidates for converting fructose to acetic acid. For cider vinegar, you can also use unpasteurized apple cider or juice purchased at your local market or fruit stand.

Fermentation of fruit to wine or cider requires humidity, darkness, and warm temperatures. You'll want to place your container in a dark basement, the pantry, or other area that receives little light and benefits from warm days and nights. If you use an air conditioner, be sure to keep your vinegar container in a protected area away from temperature fluctuations.

EQUIPMENT

Like other methods of food processing, vinegar making requires sanitary conditions and a few specialized pieces of equipment. For the most part, you may be able to use what you have at hand for making vinegar rather than purchasing extra equipment. Be sure that your utensils and equipment are sanitary. When in doubt, sterilize! Avoid the use of metal containers; the acid in the fermenting solution will discolor your container, cause corrosion, and contaminate the whole process.

Use a large glass jar, a crock, or barrel for the fermentation process. Just be sure that the openings are covered with a towel, a fine mesh screen, or cheesecloth while the juice ferments. This allows air to circulate while preventing harmful elements from entering the mix. While the friendly bacteria need air to reproduce, they can fall victim to airborne bacteria that work against the process, including the bacteria carried by the fruit flies which will inevitably begin to circulate around your brew.

TOOLS AND INGREDIENTS HELPFUL TO THE PROCESS OF MAKING VINEGAR

- A fruit press for squeezing the juice out of must or fruit pulp, or a juice extractor (juicer).

- An oak barrel, either lined with paraffin or not (according to the type of vinegar you wish to make). Most barrels come with a spigot, one bung hole, and a stand to help the barrel maintain its balance.

- A racking tube for transferring liquid from one container to another. However, you can achieve the same results by pouring the liquid through a sieve lined with several layers of cheesecloth. (I make vinegar in quantities of 2 to 3 quarts (1.9 to 2.8 L) at a time, so pouring isn't much of a challenge.)

- Commercial wine or malt yeast (never bread yeast) specific to the type of vinegar you wish to brew.

- Commercially produced mother if you don't wish to grow your own.

- Cheesecloth, towels, or mesh screen to cover the opening of jars and the holes in your barrel.

- Acid-testing paper.

- Dark brown glass bottles for storing mother.

- Bottles and caps for storing the finished, pasteurized vinegar.

Oak barrels are fun to use and last for years. For wine vinegar, use an unlined barrel to provide the special flavor that wood imparts—the taste will surpass anything you can purchase commercially. For cider vinegar, look for a barrel lined with paraffin. The paraffin prevents the transfer of the wood taste, to give your vinegar that true cider flavor.

If you are using a new barrel, you should treat it with soda ash and citric acid before use, following the manufacturer's instructions. This helps to harden and seal the fibers in the wood. Also, fill the barrel with water before use to balance out the volume of the wood—the barrel will leak initially, then seal, preventing further leaking once you use it for vinegar.

Once you've designated barrels or containers for your vinegar making, you may want to use them only for that purpose. While you can clean them for making other types of brew, certain flavors remain steeped in barrels and may adversely affect the flavor of your next batch of vinegar.

You'll know that your wine, juice, or cider has turned to vinegar because you'll be able to smell it! However, you can also test it using acid-testing paper which lets you know when the vinegar is set at a four percent acid content. Just place a few drops of liquid on the paper and follow the instructions for reading it. You can purchase this paper commercially.

Good quality apple cider vinegar can be made fairly easily. You'll need plenty of winter apples, a food processor or juice extractor, crocks, jars, or barrels for fermenting, and bottles for your end product.

cider vinegar

Autumn's blessing includes a rainbow of apples. The varieties are numerous, with availability dependent on your geographic area. When you are making cider, roam your local farmers' market for the winter apples that are most prolific and freshly picked. I like to blend varieties, combining a few sweet apples with tart and aromatic fruit for dimension.

Unlike recipes for other foods, cider (and vinegar) instructions come in approximates. The quantity of apples you need for juice will depend on the size, variety of apple, and the characteristic juice capacity contained per unit weight. I usually purchase 25 pounds (11.2 kg) of apples, and pulverize or press enough for 2 to 3 quarts (1.9 to 2.8 L) of juice at a time. The quantity is really up to you. Press enough apples to attain the volume of liquid you desire, then adjust the weight and apple count for future pressings.

If you are just getting acquainted with making vinegar, you may want to press enough apples for a quart (1 L) of juice. Although the process for making vinegar isn't difficult, you may use up a few quarts of juice before you attain the acid balance and the flavor you prefer.

YIELD: Approximately 2½ quarts (2.4 L) of cider vinegar

SHELF LIFE: Processed vinegar will keep indefinitely when stored away from sunlight

PROCESSING METHOD: Fermentation

INGREDIENTS

20–25	pounds (9 to 11.2 kg) of apples	
10	grams cider or wine yeast	
8	ounces (240 mL) mother for every 24 ounces (720 mL) hard cider (or, 1 part culture to 3 parts cider)	

METHOD
FROM JUICE TO CIDER

Assemble your equipment. If you plan to use gallon (3.8 L) jars or oak barrels, be sure that they are sanitary, and in the case of the oak barrel, watertight. You will want to use a container that is at least 30 percent greater in capacity than the amount of vinegar you wish to make. You will need the extra capacity to accommodate the foam once the juice begins to ferment. I use a one-gallon (3.8 L) jar for approximately 2½ quarts (2.4 L) of juice. This provides ample head space to be on the safe side.

Prepare the juice. Select a combination of sweet, tart, and aromatic winter apples. Remove the stems, and inspect the fruit for bruises or spoilage. While the apples don't need to be perfectly free from small surface blemishes, the fruit should be fresh and completely undamaged. Cut the apples into quarters, and process through a juicer or pulverize.

Ferment the juice. Transfer the juice to a large container. If you wish to accelerate the process, you can add 10 grams of cider or champagne-wine yeast to the juice. (Cider yeast will bring out more apple flavor, while the wine yeast will create an apple wine flavor.) Either yeast will activate the fermentation within five days. Otherwise, fermentation should begin within 10 days. Keep the container covered with a towel or cheesecloth, undisturbed, and at room temperature, 70 to 85°F (21 to 29°C). Allow the liquid to stand until the foaming subsides. Once this occurs, the first stage of fermentation is complete. This process converts the juice to an alcoholic state (cider), and you can allow the liquid to continue to stand. The longer it does so, the harder the cider will become.

FROM CIDER TO VINEGAR

When hard, unpasteurized cider is allowed to set, the yeast that encouraged the first fermentation will continue to reproduce and solidify, forming a scum, or mother, on the surface of the liquid. When this process occurs naturally, it can take up to six months. However, you can purchase or add a mother culture to speed up the process to render a mild vinegar within three to four months. This second stage of fermentation is called acetification, or the creation of vinegar (acetic acid).

If you plan to use an oak barrel for the second step of fermentation, you may want to drill holes near the top of the front and back faces. The barrel will come with a hole at the top, and the additional side holes will ensure good air circulation. The size of the barrel depends on the amount of vinegar you anticipate making. A one-gallon (3.8 L) barrel easily holds 3 quarts (2.8 L) of liquid. The barrel should be approximately three-quarters full for the air flow to reach the surface of the liquid and adequately keep the fermentation going.

STRAINING AND ACETIFICATION

With larger quantities of liquid, the transfer from one container to another requires a racking tube. Racking implies forcing the liquid to move from the bottom of the starter container to the second container for acetification. (For more racking instructions, see the sidebar on page 39.)

If you plan on tripling this recipe, or on making 2 to 3 gallons (7.6 to 11.4 L) of vinegar, the deeper containers are necessary, and you'll need to rack off the liquid. However, quantities of 3 quarts (2.8 L) are

Once the fermentation bubbles subside, transfer the cider from one container to another for acetification. This process is known as "racking-off."

After approximately three months, check on the acetifying liquid every two to three days. Once you can detect the scent of vinegar, your batch is ready to pasteurize.

Strain the pasteurized vinegar, and transfer into bottles for storage.

easily transferred by simply lifting the cider jar and pouring the liquid into a second jar or barrel. For pouring and straining, place a funnel over the opening to the second container, and pour in the cider.

Add the mother starter, and cover the openings to the jar or barrel with cheesecloth or a towel. The first time you make vinegar, you may wish to use glass jars. This will enable you to see the formation of the mother, and watch the progress of the fermentation process. You'll know how things look and be better able to detect any problems, such as a failure in the fermentation process and the inadequate formation of the scum. The mother should cover the entire surface of the liquid.

You should smell vinegar in approximately three to four months, and can begin to taste test the vinegar or test it with acid-testing paper at that time. Check the vinegar weekly until it reaches your desired strength. If, for any reason, it's stronger than you like, simply dilute it with a little water.

STRAINING AND STORING

Once the liquid tastes and smells like vinegar, the acetification is complete. You'll want to strain the vinegar and transfer it into bottles for future use. As you transfer the vinegar from the jar or barrel into bottles, use a strainer lined with four layers of cheesecloth to capture the scum or mother. You can then transfer the mother to a small, brown glass bottle with a little of the new vinegar, and store it for future use.

Once you separate the vinegar from the mother, you arrest further fermentation and possible spoilage. Vinegar will remain in excellent condition almost indefinitely once it's pasteurized. To pasteurize vinegar, heat it, and pour it into hot, sterilized bottles. Cap the bottle and process in a hot-water bath. The hot water should be no less than 140°F (60°C), but no more than 160°F (71°C). Use a thermometer to make sure that these temperatures are met. Remove the containers from the hot-water bath, allow to cool completely, and store at room temperature in a pantry or out of direct sunlight.

RACKING OFF

To "rack off" cider, or separate it from the sediment that usually resides at the bottom of the jar, insert one end of a plastic racking tube into the bottom of the container. Then siphon the cider with your mouth, pinching or clamping the end of the tube as soon as the liquid reaches your lips. Insert the closed tube into an empty second jar or container. Place the empty container at a height below the full container, allowing the pressure of siphoning to force the liquid from the full, higher bottle to the empty, lower one.

This tubing is a simple siphon for transferring liquid from one container to another.

wine vinegar

Since most wines are aged in wood barrels, using an oak barrel to make wine vinegar returns it to its natural home. The rounded, smooth flavor that wood imparts to wine will extend to the vinegar. You can use a crock or glass bottle for fermenting the wine, but the finished vinegar won't have quite the imbued body.

If you purchase a new barrel, treat it with soda ash and citric acid to harden and seal the wood. Suppliers of winemaking supplies can provide all the equipment you need, including instructions for prepping barrels, as well as for making vinegar (see Special Thanks on page 126). Before using the barrel, fill it with water; it will leak for a few minutes before finally sealing up. Whether you use a new, used, or reconditioned barrel, be sure to fill it and rinse it several times with boiling water. You need to completely eliminate any molds or other sources of possible contamination.

All vinegar needs a mother, and wine vinegar is no exception. You can purchase a mother starter culture, or make one from scratch. If you choose to make your own, blend equal parts of your wine with purified or bottled water in a large jar or crock. Cover with a towel or several layers of cheesecloth, and place in a warm, 70 to 85°F (21 to 29°C), spot away from any source of light. After four to five weeks you should see a layer of scum form on the surface of the liquid,

If using mother starter, 1/2 to 2/3 cup (120 to 160 mL) of starter will inoculate 1 gallon (3.8 L) of wine stock.

The transformation of wine to vinegar, even with a mother culture, requires at least three and up to six months to complete. Much of the timing depends on the complexity and nature of the wine used. Converting wine to vinegar requires patience, but little real work. You'll find the flavor benefits will linger for months after the process is complete.

Red or White Wine Vinegar

Blend wine, water, and vinegar mother according to the proportions on page 40. Blend enough solution so the volume of liquid fills your barrel or container three-quarters full. Place your container in a quiet area to prevent the barrel from being bumped or moved. Jarring the surface of the liquid will cause the mass of forming organisms to sink to the bottom of the barrel where they will suffocate, prohibiting the oxidation of alcohol. This will slow down the process and cause spoilage. Once you begin to detect the scent of vinegar, your process is well under way. Taste your vinegar after three months, allowing it time to mellow until it reaches the flavor you desire. Replace any vinegar that you remove for testing with an equal amount of diluted wine. Be careful to pour the diluted wine into the container through a funnel to avoid disturbing the mother.

PROPORTIONS FOR MIXING WINE VINEGAR STOCK

Acetobacters, the organisms that convert wine to vinegar, work best in an alcohol concentration of 10 percent. Alcohol content can vary from wine to wine. For example, a cabernet may contain 12 percent alcohol, and a sweet wine, such as sake, 14 percent. The best environment for transforming your leftover wine to vinegar involves the making of a stock, or diluting wine with bottled or spring water. Most wines need to be diluted to 10 percent before the organisms can begin their work. The standard proportions follow:

WINE ALCOHOL LEVEL	WINE	WATER	VINEGAR MOTHER
11%	6⅓	⅔	1
12%	5¾	1¼	1
13%	5⅓	1⅔	1
14%	5	2	1

To find out what one "part" is for your barrel, divide its total volume by 12: A 1-gallon (3.8 L) barrel holds 4 quarts (3.8 L), or four parts of liquid; a 2-gallon (7.6 L) barrel holds 8 quarts (7.6 L), or eight parts of liquid; and a 3-gallon (11.4 L) barrel holds 12 quarts (11.4 L), or 12 parts of liquid.

If your wine alcohol content is 14 percent, you need 5 parts (or 5 quarts [4.7 L]) of wine, 2 parts (or 2 quarts [1.9 L]) of water, and 1 part (or 1 quart [1 L]) of vinegar mother.

According to Paul Bertoli, the following guidelines should help if you plan to make large amounts of wine vinegar: Divide the total capacity of your barrel by 12. To calculate how much wine to use, multiply the amount of diluted wine you need by the desired alcohol concentration, then divide that number by the actual alcohol concentration of the wine. To find out how much water to use, subtract the wine amount from the total amount of liquid needed.

When the vinegar is to your taste, it is ready for immediate use or storage. Draw the vinegar into sterile bottles, cap or cork, and place them in storage for future use. Transferring the wine vinegar and capping it will halt the influx of air, which can affect fermentation. As your vinegar nestles into the darkness, it will gain mellow complexity over time.

Rice Wine Vinegar

Unlike most wines, sake, which is the national wine of Japan, requires no aging. This yellow, sweet beverage is served warm, and usually carries a fairly low alcohol content. Rice wine, as well as its vinegar, has a myriad of uses in Japanese as well as other Asian cuisine. This vinegar is fairly simply to make and follows the basic procedures for making other varieties of wine vinegar.

Sake contains 14 percent alcohol, and, like other wines, needs to be diluted before blending with a mother for acetification. Follow the blending proportions in the chart on the left. Make and store rice wine vinegar as you would any other red or white wine vinegar. Just remember that the scent and flavor remain the true deciding factors for its readiness in the kitchen or for the pantry.

vertjuice

The French initiated the term vinegar as we know it today. It derives from *vin aigre*, or "sour wine," and alludes to vinegar as a distinct by-product of the winemaking industry. The vinegar that developed before the birth of Christ was followed by *vertjuice* (also know as *verjus*) or "green juice" in the Middle Ages. Made from unripe fruit, this vinegar evolved when French peasants couldn't attain ripe fruit during the grape harvest. This vinegar gained wide popularity in the 16th century when vineyard owners finally allowed the harvest of the second growth of unripe grapes. Today, home cooks still make vertjus from the unripe fruit of white, red, and black grapes. Although this kitchen craft began with wine grapes, it is acceptable to use any grape variety.

give me some sugar

Some fruits have ample sugar for attaining the five percent alcohol content required for good vinegar. Winter apples, for example, contain sugar in excess of 10 percent. Grapes contain even higher sugar levels, therefore yielding higher alcohol levels, and creating a stronger vinegar. Plums, berries, peaches, citrus fruits, and herbs do not contain sugar levels sufficient for making vinegar. However, you can use them to infuse hot, distilled vinegar, which marries the acetic tang to the flavor of the fruit or herb.

pineapple vinegar

Once you make pineapple vinegar, you'll find at least a dozen uses for it. Its tropical personality and smooth, tangy flavor invite their way into salsa, chilies, stews, and creamy sauces. This recipe is an adaptation of that presented by Diana Kennedy, one of our foremost authorities on Mexican cuisine. This recipe is simple, requiring only good fruit, sunlight, and time.

YIELD: 2 quart (1L) jars
SHELF LIFE: 6 months after processing
PROCESSING METHOD: Fermentation
PROCESSING TIME: 15 minutes in a hot-water bath

INGREDIENTS

2½ quarts (2.4 L) white distilled water

1 cup (145 g) dark brown sugar, packed

2 slices of pineapple, cut lengthwise to measure approximately ½ inch (1.3 cm) thick and 4 inches (10 cm) long with the skin on

EQUIPMENT

1 one-gallon (3.8 L) glass jar

METHOD

Blend the water and the sugar in the jar and add the pineapple slices. Cover the jar with plastic wrap, and place in a sunny spot on your kitchen counter or on the top of your stove. Just be sure that the liquid receives a fairly constant temperature regardless of location. Temperatures of 72 to 80°F (22 to 26°C) are best for fermentation.

The liquid should begin to froth and bubble after seven days. Once the bubbling begins, leave the pineapple slices in the liquid for another 10 days. Remove the fruit and allow the fermentation process to continue. The liquid will continue to bubble for another three to four weeks.

Once the fermentation process has subsided, strain the vinegar into a medium saucepan. Bring the vinegar to a boil over medium heat, and allow it to cook for 10 minutes. The vinegar will quickly reduce in volume. Pour the hot liquid into hot, sterilized jars, apply the caps, and process for 15 minutes in a hot-water bath. The temperature of the water should be no less than 140°F (60°C), and no more than 160°F (71°C). Use a thermometer to monitor the water temperature while processing. Remove the jars from the hot-water bath, and set aside to cool to room temperature. Store the vinegar in a dark pantry or kitchen area away from the sunlight.

FRUIT-INFUSED VINEGAR

A countless array of fruits and herbs yield pleasantly to vinegar infusion. This recipe is quick, requiring only cold vinegar and berries. Once steeped with juice, the vinegar can be diluted with sparkling water for a refreshing summer drink, or used with oil and other seasonings for salads and marinades. Your imagination is the path to discovery.

YIELD: 1 quart (1L) jar

INGREDIENTS

    3 cups (448 g) of red raspberries or blueberries
        White distilled vinegar

METHOD

Rinse and clean your berries, removing any small stems. Set aside in a colander to drain

Place the berries in a sterilized jar and pour the vinegar over them. Apply the lid, adjust the cap, and allow the mixture to stand for 10 days in a cool, quiet area of your kitchen or pantry.

Strain the vinegar from the berries, and transfer to another jar. Refrigerate for future use.

fish & chips

While crispy fried cod and crunchy potatoes make up the heart of fish and chips, vinegar claims its soul. Sometime during 1864, the London shopkeeper Joseph Malines created a rage when he decided to offer his customers fried fish and potatoes liberally doused with hearty malt vinegar. The fare gained in popularity when fisherman found that they could chill large quantities of fish from the North Sea on ice, bring it back to port, and deliver fresh goods. Englishmen as well as their visitors took a strong liking to the deep-fried combination that was wrapped in the daily newspaper. Over 150 years later, fish and chips continues as standard pub fare throughout England, and graces many a menu in North America as well.

the pickle recipes

CHIPOTLES IN ADOBO SAUCE

YIELD: 4 half-pint (.25 L) jars, or 2 pint (.5 L) jars

SHELF LIFE: Without processing, refrigerated for 3–5 days. With processing, up to 6 months

PROCESSING METHOD: Hot pack; hot-water bath, or fresh for immediate use

HEAD SPACE: ½ inch (1.3 cm) for hot pack only

PROCESSING TIME: 20 minutes

There are chipotles, and there is adobo sauce...and then there are chipotles in adobo sauce. The chipotle, revered as an eye-watering, smoked jalapeño, takes on a whole new dimension when immersed in the sweet-hot tang of adobo, or barbecue sauce. The chilies and the sauce can be found as separate specialty items at the market; they usually come in small cans that carry a big cost.

While you need to start with a large quantity of peppers, followed by smoking them to reduce them to a somewhat shriveled state, the results will fatten your pantry with an ingredient that's essential to Mexican and southwestern cuisine—at a fraction of the supermarket price.

This recipe calls for smoking 10 pounds (4.5 kg) of jalapeño chilies to yield about 1 to 1½ pounds (448 to 672 g) of chipotles. You'll want to process them in half-pint or pint (.25 to .5 L) jars, remembering that a chipotle or two provides the seasoning for an entire batch of enchiladas or a pot of chili.

NOTE: *This recipe calls for processing the chipotle in adobo sauce. However, if you just want to use the chipotles alone, smoke the peppers, allow them to cool, and place them in air-tight plastic bags or containers to store in your pantry for future use.*

INGREDIENTS

- 10 pounds fresh jalapeño peppers
- 2 cups (480 mL) white distilled vinegar
- 1/2 teaspoon salt
- 1/4 cup (35 g) light brown sugar, loosely packed
- 1/2 teaspoon cumin
- 1/4 teaspoon marjoram
- 1/4 teaspoon cinnamon
- 6 garlic cloves, peeled
- 3 cloves, whole

SMOKE THE PEPPERS

In Mexico, jalapeños are traditionally smoked on a rack above a fiery pit, which serves as a point of convergence for underground tunnels that direct air to the fire. This casts clouds of billowing smoke upward, which greets the chilies as they are roasting away. Since the fire is neither high nor extremely hot, the process of smoking is mellow, steady, and time consuming.

Barring access to a fire pit, smoke the jalapeños with a meat smoker or kettle grill. Select plump, moist jalapeños for best results. Be sure that your grill is thoroughly clean and free from any particles of meat or other grilled food prior to smoking the chipotles. Any residue from previously cooked food will waft into your chilies and change their flavor.

Smoke the jalapeños over a wood fire. Be selective about the type of wood-smoked flavor you choose. Fruit-tree wood, as well as hardwood, such as oak,

pecan, and hickory, create wonderful smoked flavors. We have used pecan wood, along with a few pecan shells for added dimension.

Place two small mounds of charcoal briquettes on either side of the base of the grill. Soak the wood in water before placing it on the coals. The intent here is to create a steady, ongoing path of heat and smoke without high flame. If necessary, open or adjust the vents at the base of the grill for additional ventilation.

While the coals are heating, wash the jalapeños, remove the stems, and pat dry. Discard any peppers with nicks, scratches, or bruises. Place the jalapeños on a mesh rack and allow them to smoke until they are dark brown, shriveled, and somewhat hard. Discard any peppers that look badly charred.

Depending on the humidity of your climate, the smoking process can take 8 to 12 hours, or perhaps more. Once your peppers are smoked, they become chipotles, ready for adobo or barbecue sauce. Transfer them from the grill to a large pan, and set aside.

MAKE THE SAUCE

Place the vinegar, salt, sugar, cumin, marjoram, cinnamon, garlic, and cloves in a food processor or blender. Pulse until the ingredients form a smooth sauce. Transfer the sauce to a medium saucepan. Bring the ingredients to a boil, reduce the heat, and allow the sauce to simmer for 5 minutes. Add the chipotles and blend, making sure the sauce coats all of the peppers.

Pack the hot chipotles in sauce into hot, sterilized jars, leaving 1/2 inch for head room. Use a bubble freer to release any excess air. Process for 20 minutes in a hot water bath. Remove the jars from the bath and allow to cool in a draft-free area before storing.

MAUI MARINADE

The old-world culinary trilogy of sweetness, heat, and spice embraces this dish with garlic, lime, and chilies, offering modern kitchens an irresistible combination of tastes. Make a jar or two for the pantry, or use fresh. Since chilies are available in most markets throughout the winter, cooking a batch of marinade for immediate use will offer a delightful change of pace in colder weather. However, if you plan to process for storage, use in-season produce at the peak of freshness.

YIELD: Approximately 2 pint (.5 L) jars
SHELF LIFE: In the refrigerator, 1 week. With processing, up to 6 months
PROCESSING METHOD: Hot pack; hot-water bath
HEAD SPACE: ½ inch (1.3 cm)
PROCESSING TIME: 15 minutes in a hot-water bath

INGREDIENTS

½ cup (120 mL) white wine vinegar

½ cup (120 mL) white distilled vinegar

1 cup (240 mL) soy sauce

½ teaspoon fine black pepper

½ cup (170 g) light corn oil

6 tablespoons (30 g) light brown sugar

3 cloves fresh garlic, peeled and minced

3 tablespoons ginger, peeled and minced

4–5 small serrano peppers, seeded, stemmed, and minced

Zest of two limes

METHOD

In a small saucepan, blend all of the ingredients with a whisk. Bring the mixture to a boil over medium heat, reduce the heat, and allow the liquid to bubble for another 10 minutes.

For refrigerator storage, remove from the heat and allow to cool to room temperature. Transfer the marinade to a lidded container and place in the refrigerator.

For the pantry, pour the hot marinade into hot sterilized jars, leaving ½ inch (1.3 cm) head room. Apply the lids, adjust the caps, and process in a hot-water bath for 15 minutes. Remove the jars and allow them to cool in a draft-free area before storing.

PICKLED GINGER

Long touted for its medicinal properties, ginger has offered its benefits to the circulatory, digestive, and respiratory systems. I always thought that ginger was excellent when simmered for tea. And of course, it's a mainstay when baking. But pickled? Once you've tried a bit of pickled ginger with fish or grilled meats, you'll find a reason to use it raw as well as cooked. It complements Japanese cuisine with an unmistakable flair. Look for fresh, young ginger in December and January when the skin is thin and easy to remove and the flesh easy to slice.

YIELD: 2 half-pint (.25 L) jars
SHELF LIFE: Up to one year
PROCESSING METHOD: Cold pack; hot-water bath
HEAD SPACE: ½ inch (1.3 cm)
PROCESSING TIME: 10 minutes in a hot-water bath

INGREDIENTS

- ½ pound (224 g) fresh young ginger
- 1 tablespoon kosher salt
- 1½ cups (360 mL) rice wine vinegar, of the highest quality
- 1 tablespoon soy sauce
- 1 tablespoon water
- ¼ cup (50 g) granulated sugar
- 1 teaspoon salt

METHOD

Lightly scrape the ginger with a potato peeler, being careful to remove the skin, but not too much of the flesh. Using a very sharp knife, or vegetable cutter, shave the ginger into paper-thin slices.

Place the sliced ginger in a small bowl, add the kosher salt, and rub it into the ginger until you can't feel the salt against your fingers. Cover and seal the bowl with plastic wrap, and refrigerate overnight.

Remove the bowl from the refrigerator. Gently squeeze the ginger, a little at a time, to drain any liquid and excess salt from the slices. Pack the ginger into hot sterilized jars.

In a small saucepan, bring the rice wine vinegar, soy sauce, water, sugar, and salt to a boil. Pour the liquid over the ginger. Release any excess air with a bubble freer. Apply the lids, adjust the caps, and process for 10 minutes in a hot-water bath. Remove the jars and set aside to cool in a draft-free area before storing.

NOTE: *If you wish to store the ginger in the refrigerator without processing, simply pour the hot liquid into the jars, release the excess air, and allow the jars to cool completely. Seal and refrigerate. Your ginger will keep well for 3 to 4 weeks.*

YIELD: 2 pint (.5 L) jars

SHELF LIFE: In the refrigerator, 1 week. With processing, up to 6 months

PROCESSING METHOD: Hot pack; hot-water bath

HEAD SPACE: ½ inch (1.3 cm)

PROCESSING TIME: 20 minutes in a hot-water bath

GOLDEN PASTA SAUCE

Combine the rich warm hues of yellow and orange bell peppers with a tomato or two. Then add herbs, vinegar, and a touch of olive oil to make a pasta sauce that retains excellent color and flavor. This sauce can be cooked and kept in the refrigerator, or processed and stored in your pantry for those days that invite respite from the chill of winter. I always enjoy adding this sauce to a housewarming basket, along with crusty bread, a bag of pasta, fruit, and cheese. You'll find the recipe doubles and even triples accurately. However, no matter how much you make, always process the recipe in smaller jars; it will retain better color and flavor than processing in larger quart (1 L) jars.

INGREDIENTS

4 yellow bell peppers, roasted, peeled, and seeded

2 orange bell peppers, roasted, peeled, and seeded

3 yellow or 4 red medium plum tomatoes, halved, seeded, and roasted

¼ cup (12.5 g) fresh lemon basil

1 tablespoon lemon zest

¼ cup (60 mL) olive oil

4 cloves garlic, peeled and chopped

¼ cup (60 mL) white distilled vinegar

¼ cup (60 mL) white balsamic vinegar

½ teaspoon salt

¼ teaspoon ground black pepper|

METHOD

Preheat the oven to 500°F (260°C).

Remove the stems and seeds from the peppers and tomatoes. Gently pierce the wall of each pepper with the tip of a sharp knife, allowing hot air to escape (preventing explosions) during roasting. Place the peppers and tomatoes on a cookie sheet, and roast on the middle rack of the oven for 30 minutes, or until the skins turn dark brown and swell away from the flesh. Remove the cookie sheet from the oven. Using a pair of tongs, transfer the peppers to a paper or plastic bag. Seal the bag, and allow the peppers to stand for 20 minutes. Remove the peppers from the bag, and slip off the charred skins.

Transfer the tomatoes to a blender. Add the basil, lemon zest, olive oil, garlic, vinegars, salt, and pepper. Pulse until the ingredients are smoothly blended. Add the roasted peppers, one at a time, and pulse until all of the ingredients blend into a thick sauce. Transfer the sauce to a medium saucepan, and cook over medium heat for 15 minutes.

For use within seven days, transfer the sauce immediately to a small container, and allow the sauce to cool to room temperature. Cover and refrigerate.

For processing, pour the hot sauce into hot sterilized jars, leaving ½ inch (1.3 cm) head room. Apply the lids, adjust the caps, and process in a hot-water bath for 20 minutes. Remove and allow to cool in a draft-free area before storing.

PRESERVED LEMONS

Whether you slice them, chop them, or use them whole, preserved lemons lend a mellow citrus-sweet tang to foods. I use them chopped in salsa, whole in soup, and sliced or quartered for casseroles and tagines. Despite the dimensions of their exotic flavor, the steps for pickling lemons remain utterly simple. Once you've preserved a lemon or two, you'll want to keep a few jars on hand. This recipe also halves easily if you wish to make a smaller batch.

YIELD: 1 quart (1 L) jar, approximately 8–10 lemons
SHELF LIFE: Up to 6 months in the refrigerator
PROCESSING METHOD: Salting and curing
HEAD SPACE: $1/2$ inch (1.3 cm)
PROCESSING TIME: Cure for 14 days, then refrigerate

INGREDIENTS

8–10 medium lemons with unblemished smooth, thin skins

$1\frac{1}{2}$–$1\frac{3}{4}$ cups (300–350 g) kosher salt

2 tablespoons sugar

1 cup (240 mL) freshly squeezed lemon juice. (Never use reconstituted or bottled juice.)

METHOD

Select 8 to 10 perfect lemons, free from any scratches, bruises, or dark spots on their skin. Wash and dry the lemons with a lint-free towel. Using a sharp knife, cut a thin slice from the top and bottom of each lemon. Stand one lemon on end, then cut it three-quarters of the way through so the two halves remain attached at the base. Turn the lemon 90°, then cut it the same way. This will make quarters that remain attached at the base. Do this with all the lemons.

Blend the salt and sugar in a small bowl. Spoon the mixture into the lemons by holding the lemon open with one hand, then packing as much salt and sugar as each lemon will hold. Put the lemon in the bottom of a cooled, sterilized quart jar. Pack a second lemon with the salt and sugar blend, and place it into the jar. Continue stuffing and packing the lemons on top of each other, pressing them down as you fill the jar. It's important to press or squeeze the lemons so they will release additional juice for the curing process.

Once all of the lemons have been pressed into the jar, pour in the freshly squeezed lemon juice until all of the lemons are covered. Leave $1/2$ inch (1.3 cm) of head room. Apply the lid and adjust the cap on the jar. Place it in a dark, cool pantry or similar area in your kitchen. Allow the lemons to cure for 14 days. During the curing time, turn the sealed jar upside down, then right side up every 24 hours. This turning ensures all the lemons will be saturated with the juice while they cure. After 14 days, your lemons are ready to use or refrigerate for future recipes. The juice in the jar will probably be a bit thick. Rinse the lemons slightly before use.

CURED OLIVES

As wine growers continue to flourish worldwide, they also tend to cultivate groves of olives along with their grapes. The right balance of sunshine, warm nights, and humidity work magic for both fruits. Some of us are fortunate to live near the hillsides which spawn the wine and olives we enjoy throughout the year. Once you taste a home-cured olive, you'll begin to look for reasons to visit a grove during the early fall.

The recipes here have been generously shared by long-time olive lovers and friends, Don and Olga Cossi. They have traveled up and down the west coast of America, selecting fresh olives from the harvest for home curing. I've received a number of packages over the years containing tasty homemade green or black

olives seasoned with garlic and herbs. Green and black olives need to be cured separately, but afterwards you can mix them or layer them into your favorite flavor combinations.

The recipes call for soaking olives in a lye and water solution that provides the strong alkaline base needed for firming and preserving the meat of the olive, while curing it at the same time. The curing process involves several days. You will first treat the olives in the lye solution, soak them to refresh them, then brine them in salt. To help you better plan your time during the curing process, I've divided the total curing time into day-by-day steps. Since each step involves a few hours, it's best to get started in the morning.

GREEN RIPE OLIVES

INGREDIENTS

8–10 pounds (3.6 to 4.8 kg) olives

   1 12-ounce can (336 g) flake lye

   6 gallons (22.6 L) water

METHOD

CAUTION: *Use extreme caution when blending water and lye. The chemical reaction creates a hot and tempestuous fluid. It's best to wear gloves and eye protection. Make sure that your skin, particularly on your arms, is well protected. Work slowly and carefully when stirring the lye into the water to avoid as many splashes and spills as possible. Only use glass or stoneware containers, and stir with a wooden spoon or glass rod. Never use an aluminum container; the lye will ruin it. Never use a galvanized metal container because the lye will dissolve the zinc, allowing it to penetrate your olives and cause a poisonous reaction.*

DAYS 1 AND 2

Look for fresh, firm, green or red olives that are free from scratches, nicks, or bruises. Wash, drain, and set aside.

Add 4 tablespoons, or 2 ounces (56 g), of lye per each gallon (3.8 L) of water. Slowly and carefully add the lye to the water. Stir the solution with a wooden spoon or glass rod until the lye has completely dissolved. The chemical reaction will create a bubbling hot solution. This solution needs to stand until it cools to a temperature of 65 to 70°F (18 to 21°C).

Place the olives in a large glass bowl or crock. Add the lye solution until all of them are immersed. Cover with a towel or a cloth to make sure the olives stay submerged. Throughout the curing process, they must remain submerged. Long exposure to air will darken your olives.

Stir the olives every three hours with a wooden spoon or glass rod so that the lye can circulate around the fruit, penetrate it, and reach the pits. During this soaking time, you will also start to check the olives for softening every two to three hours. To check them, press them with the end of a wooden spoon. The olives are ready for the next step when they are no longer hard, and the flesh yields easily to the pressure of the spoon.

TOTAL CURING TIME: 12–14 days

YIELD: Approximately 8–10 pint (.5 L) jars, or 4–5 quart (1 L) jars

SHELF LIFE: After brining, 6–12 months for best flavor

PROCESSING METHOD: Brining

Just before draining this batch, it's good to test the olives for softening one more time. If they are still harder than you like, let them soak for one more hour. If you think they are soft enough, remove a few olives, rinse them, and cut them to the pit with a sharp knife. The flesh should yield easily, and should be a pale yellow-green. (Fresh, untreated olives are deeper and brighter in color.)

Drain the olives, carefully discarding the lye solution. Rinse the olives twice under cold tap water, draining the olives after each rinse. Cover the olives with cold water.

DAYS 3 TO 10

Each day, change the water covering the olives. Each change will draw more lye solution out of the fruit. After day 10, taste a few olives. You will not want to taste any residual lye. If necessary, change the water for an extra day or two. Be aware that the extra changes of water will extend the total curing time to 14 days.

DAYS 11 AND 12

Prepare a salt brine by blending 4 ounces (112 g) of kosher salt to every gallon (3.8 L) of water you will need for covering the olives. Submerge the olives in the brine, and allow the olives to stand for another two days. Rinse and store the olives in the refrigerator. If you plan on using the olives immediately, you'll want to soak them in plain water to remove any excess saltiness.

If you plan on keeping the olives for longer than two weeks, you'll need to create another brine. To do this, blend 8 ounces (224 g) of kosher salt per gallon (3.8 L) of water. Store the olives in this brine for one week. Drain the brine and rinse the olives. Place the olives in a fresh brine made of 1 pound (448 g) salt per gallon (3.8 L) of water. Allow the olives to soak for 10 days, then repeat using a brine of 1 pound (448 g) salt per gallon (3.8 L) of water. The olives will keep in this last brine until you are ready to eat them. At that time, soak the olives overnight in plain water before consuming.

BLACK OLIVES

This process also starts with fresh green or red olives. The fruit undergoes four treatments of lye, which preserves and darkens the fruit to dark brown or black. After you have completed the four treatments of lye, you will rinse and brine your dark olives following the same guidelines for brining and storing green olives.

TOTAL CURING TIME: 19–21 days
YIELD: 8–9 pint (.5 L) jars, or 4–5 quart (1 L) jars
SHELF LIFE: After brining, 6–12 months for best flavor
PROCESSING METHOD: Brining

INGREDIENTS

8–10 pounds (3.6–4.8 kg) olives
1 12-ounce can (336 g) flake lye
6 gallons (22.8 L) water

DAYS 1 AND 2

Look for fresh, firm, green or red olives that are free from scratches, nicks, or bruises. Wash, drain, and set aside. Add 3 tablespoons, or $1^1/_2$ ounces (42 g), of lye per each gallon (3.8 L) of water. Slowly and carefully add the lye to the water. Stir with a wooden spoon or glass rod until all of the lye dissolves, then allow the solution to cool to 65 to 70°F (18 to 21°C).

Pour the lye solution over the olives, and allow them to soak for 10 to 12 hours. Cover them with a towel or cloth to keep them submerged in the solution. During this soaking time, you will start checking the olives for softening. After the olives have soaked for 3 hours, start to check them by pressing them with the end of a wooden spoon. Continue to check them this way every 30 minutes. The olives are ready for the next step when they are no longer hard, and the flesh yields easily to the pressure of the spoon. Once they are soft, drain off the lye solution, and allow the olives to sit exposed to the air in the bowl or crock for 8 to 10 hours. Gently stir the olives occasionally to make sure that air gets to all of the fruit.

DAYS 3 AND 4

Make another lye solution from $1^1/_2$ ounces (42 g) of lye per gallon (3.8 L) of boiling water. Pour the solution over the olives and allow them to soak for another 8 hours. Drain off the solution, and allow the olives to sit exposed to air for another day, stirring them occasionally.

DAYS 5 AND 6

Repeat the steps for the second lye treatment.

DAYS 7 AND 8

Repeat the steps for the third lye treatment.

DAY 9

Drain the olives, carefully discarding the lye solution. Rinse the olives twice under cold tap water, draining the olives after each rinse. Cover the olives with cold water.

DAYS 10 TO 17

The next day, and each day after that, change the water covering the olives. Each change will draw more lye solution out of the fruit. After day 17, taste a few olives. You will not want to taste any residual lye. If necessary, change the water for an extra day or two. Be aware that the extra changes of water will extend the total curing time to 21 days.

DAYS 18 AND 19

Follow the same brining and storage instructions for the green olives listed under Days 11 and 12 for that recipe.

PICKLED GARLIC

East meets west when your kitchen houses garlic in all of its states: raw, dried, powdered, frozen, and even pickled. As I came to understand the subtleties and powers of Korean food, I found that pickled garlic offered a unique flavor dimension to Asian dishes—tart, a little hot, and lingering. When you pickle a pint or two, you'll discover an open door to Eastern cuisine—where garlic more than likely got its start in the kitchen.

If you want to pickle whole heads of garlic, go to your garden or farmers' market during the late spring or early summer when the heads are immature and free from the outer papery layer. Otherwise, you can pickle the peeled cloves. If you ever want to play, pickle individual cloves of elephant garlic (which is really a leek).

YIELD: 2 half-pint (.25 L) jars
SHELF LIFE: Up to 12 months
PROCESSING METHOD: Fermentation
HEAD SPACE: ½ inch (1.3 cm)

INGREDIENTS

- 6–8 small bulbs of garlic, each approximately 1¼ inches (3 cm) in diameter
- 1 cup (240 mL) soy sauce
- ¾ cup (180 mL) rice wine vinegar
- ¼ cup (60 mL) white distilled vinegar
- ¼ cup (50 g) granulated sugar
- 1 teaspoon kosher or pickling salt

METHOD

Trim the stem ends from the garlic and remove any excess fiber from the root end. With your thumb and fingertips, gently rub away any excess dirt or soil. Rinse the garlic under cool water. Inspect the garlic for any dark spot, bruises, or openings of the remaining skin or flesh. Discard and replace any damaged bulbs. If you are pickling individual cloves, separate the cloves from the bulb and peel them. Put the cleaned garlic in a small bowl and set aside.

Place the soy sauce, rice vinegar, white distilled vinegar, sugar, and salt in a blender. Pulse until all of the ingredients are blended. Pour the liquid over the garlic, and gently toss until all of the bulbs or cloves are coated. Cover the container with a towel, and allow it to stand in a cool, dark place for 48 hours.

Using a pair of tongs or slotted spoon, place the garlic bulbs or cloves in the jars. Pour the remaining liquid into a small saucepan and bring it to a boil. Reduce the heat, and allow the liquid to simmer until it is reduced to nearly half. Remove the pan from the heat, and set aside to cool.

Pour the liquid over the garlic to allow ½ inch (1.3 cm) of head room. Using a bubble freer, release any additional air in the jars. Apply the lids, adjust the caps, and place the jars in a dark, cool spot (your pantry) for 3 to 4 weeks. After that time, your pickled garlic is ready to serve—slice it, eat it like a pickle, or add it to your next Asian recipe.

TOMATO PEACH SALSA

Creating new and intriguing flavor combinations for salsa seems to have grown to a tradition in ethnic and nouvelle cuisine. What originally began as a spicy blend of tomatoes, peppers, and onions has expanded to include pineapple, mango, peaches, and citrus fruits. If you plan to take advantage of the harvest, your experience just won't be complete without a jar or two of salsa. This blend of tomatoes and peaches serves as an excellent side, or as a basting sauce for grilled foods. You can, of course, make it and use it immediately, but it also keeps well for several months in the pantry after processing.

YIELD: 2 pint (.5 L) jars

SHELF LIFE: Up to 6 months for best flavor and color

PROCESSING METHOD: Cold pack; hot-water bath

HEAD SPACE: 1/2 inch (1.3 m)

PROCESSING TIME: 15 minutes in a hot-water bath

INGREDIENTS

2 3/4 cups (560 g) fresh peaches, peeled and coarsely chopped (approximately 5 medium peaches)

3/4 cup (168 g) ripe plum tomatoes, seeded and coarsely chopped (approximately 4 medium plum tomatoes)

1/3 cup (65 g) granulated sugar

1/3 cup (35 g) light brown sugar, loosely packed

1/3 cup (80 mL) white distilled vinegar

1 tablespoon jalapeño chili, seeded and minced

1 teaspoon crushed dried red chili

2 cloves garlic, peeled and pressed

1 teaspoon kosher salt

1/2 teaspoon black ground pepper

METHOD

Combine all of the ingredients in a medium bowl, cover tightly with plastic wrap, and refrigerate for 8 to 10 hours or overnight. Use fresh, or process.

To process for pantry storage, ladle the salsa into hot sterilized jars, leaving 1/2 inch (1.3 cm) of head room. Apply the lids, adjust the caps, and process for 15 minutes in a hot-water bath. Remove the jars and set them aside to seal in a draft-free area before storing.

TOMATILLOS AND JALAPEÑOS

This spicy blend of little Mexican green tomatoes and chilies keeps well for months in your pantry. Use them for enchiladas, sauces, or as a side of pickled fare to your favorite southwestern salad. Peppers are among the easiest pickles to make, and this recipe stands well for short- and long-term storage.

YIELD: 3 quart (1 L) jars
SHELF LIFE: For the refrigerator, 3–4 weeks. With processing, up to 6 months
PROCESSING METHOD: Cold pack; hot-water bath
HEAD SPACE: ½ inch (1.3 m)
PROCESSING TIME: 10 minutes in a hot-water bath

INGREDIENTS

1½ pounds (672 g) jalapeños (approximately 30)

1½ pounds (672 g) tomatillos (approximately 30)

1 teaspoon kosher salt per quart (1 L) jar

12 cloves of garlic, peeled

12 sprigs fresh oregano

12 leaves lemon mint

3 bay leaves, whole

6–8 cups (1.5–1.9 L) white distilled vinegar, boiling hot

METHOD

Remove the papery husks from the tomatillos, rinse, pat dry, and set aside. Cut away the outer stems from the jalapeños, rinse, and pat dry.

Spoon the salt into the hot sterilized jars. Distribute the garlic, oregano, mint, and bay leaves among the jars. Pierce the skin of each of the peppers and tomatillos with the tip of a sharp knife, then arrange them in layers in the jars.

For the refrigerator, pour the boiling hot vinegar into the jars, release any excess air with a bubble freer, apply the lids, and adjust the caps. Allow the jars to cool, undisturbed, in a draft-free area before transferring to the refrigerator.

For processing for the pantry, pour the hot vinegar into the jars, allowing ½ inch (1.3 m) of head room, and release any excess air with a bubble freer. Apply the lids, adjust the caps, and process for 10 minutes in a hot-water bath. Remove the jars and allow them to cool in a draft-free area before storing.

YIELD: 1 pound (448 g)

SHELF LIFE: 2–3 months in the refrigerator when tightly wrapped

PROCESSING METHOD: Brining and curing

PROCESSING: 1 day for heating and ripening curds, 5 days for curing the finished cheese

FETA IN SALT BRINE

Historically called "pickled cheese," feta is best known for its tangy addition to Greek salads and Middle Eastern cuisine. Feta supplies a bounty of nutrition, and is traditionally made from sheep's or goat's milk. Look for quality goat's milk in whole-foods markets. It comes pasteurized, so you only need to warm it up to get things started.

   Feta cheese requires a day for making and draining curds. However, you won't be in the kitchen much due to the waiting time between steps. Once you salt your cheese, then refrigerate it in an airtight container for five days, you'll taste a feta that will spoil you for most commercial varieties.

INGREDIENTS

   1   gallon (3.84 L) whole goat's milk

1¼   teaspoons mesophilic starter

   1   teaspoon liquid calf's rennet, blended with
        ¼ cup (60 mL) of cool water

   4   tablespoons flake salt

METHOD

In a double boiler, warm the milk over medium heat for approximately 15 to 20 minutes, or until the temperature reaches 85°F (29°C). At this temperature, add the mesophilic starter and blend with a wire whisk. Remove the double boiler from the heat, cover it, and allow the milk to ripen for 1 hour.

Lift the pot of ripened milk out of the double boiler and set aside. Blend the rennet with the water, and add this liquid to the ripened milk. Gently stir the milk so that the rennet is evenly distributed. Cover the pot and allow the rennet to work for approximately 1 hour. To test, cut the curd with a knife. If no curd clings to the knife, you are ready for the next step.

Cut the curds into ¾-inch (1.9 cm) cubes, and allow the entire mass to rest for 20 minutes. This cutting and resting releases the curds from the whey, which will rise to the surface as the cheese sits. In the next 30 minutes, gently stir the curds several times to keep them separated and to work off any extra whey.

Ladle the curds into a colander lined with a double thickness of cheesecloth. Make sure that the cheesecloth is large enough to allow you to tie the ends together to form a draining bag for the curds. Tie the ends together, and slip a dowel or chopstick underneath the knot. Hang the bag, supported by the dowel or chopstick, inside the cheese pot for draining.

Allow the curds to hang for approximately 5 hours, or until the whey has completely dripped off the cheesecloth bag. At this point, you should be able to feel a firm, solid mass of curds. If you can't, allow the curds to drain for another hour, then check for firmness again.

Untie the bag and transfer the feta to a large bowl. Cut the cheese into slices, each approximately 1¼ inches (3 cm) thick, then into ¼-inch (.6 cm) cubes. Sprinkle the feta with the flake salt, making sure that all surfaces are covered.

Loosely cover the bowl with a sheet of plastic wrap, top with a towel, and allow the curds to steep in the flake salt in the refrigerator for 5 days. At this time, the feta is ready to use. Transfer the feta along with the brine to an airtight container and store in the refrigerator until ready to serve.

PURPLE PICKLED EGGS

While eggs can be pickled right along with beets, it's fun to treat them as a stand-alone item. This recipe calls for first preparing pickled beet juice enhanced with spice, which will penetrate the eggs with a rosy glow.

YIELD: 1 quart (1 L)
SHELF LIFE: Use fresh after steeping the eggs
PROCESSING METHOD: Refrigerator pickle
HEAD SPACE: None required
PROCESSING TIME: None required

INGREDIENTS

1–1½ cups (240–360 mL) fresh beet juice from three beets (see below)

1 cup (240 mL) distilled white vinegar

1 teaspoon pickling salt

1 bay leaf, left whole

1 pinch dried tarragon

1 teaspoon pickling spice

10–12 hard-cooked eggs, peeled and left whole

METHOD

For the beet juice, select three beets, each approximately 2 inches (5 cm) in diameter. Leave the beets whole, with approximately 1½ inches (3.8 cm) of the stems attached. Place the beets in a small saucepan with 2½ cups (600 mL) of water, and bring to a boil. Allow the beets to cook for 10 minutes, or until tender when pierced with a knife. Remove the beets and set aside for another use, or discard. Through a funnel lined with cheesecloth, strain the beet juice into a measuring cup or bowl and set aside.

Place the beet juice, vinegar, salt, bay leaf, dried tarragon, and pickling spice in a medium saucepan, and bring to a low boil. Simmer for 4 to 5 minutes, then remove from the heat, and set aside to cool until the liquid is close to room temperature. Gently place the eggs in the jar, then pour the liquid over them. Cover the jar tightly with a nonreactive cap, and refrigerate for at least 8 to 10 hours. If you wish to serve the eggs without discolored yolks, serve or use within 24 hours.

PLUM TOMATOES GENOVESE

Whole, meaty plum tomatoes are good candidates for the dryer, as well as the hot-water-bath canner. When halved and dried, their flavor solidifies into a chewy mouthful for pizza or antipasto. When packed and processed with garlic, Genovese basil, and a little wine vinegar, they offer a great base for sauce and soups. Once generally thought of as a high-acid food, tomatoes are now classified as a low-acid food. However, they are still perfectly safe for processing in a hot-water bath. Choose tomatoes that are firm and ripe, avoiding soft or juicy specimens.

YIELD: 4 pint (.5 L) jars
SHELF LIFE: 3–4 months
PROCESSING METHOD:
   Cold pack; hot-water bath
HEAD SPACE: ½ inch (1.3 cm)
PROCESSING TIME: 30 minutes

Remember to always use an altitude chart (see page 26) for the amount of processing time required in your geographic area.

INGREDIENTS

24–36 firm plum tomatoes

1 tablespoon pickling salt

1 teaspoon sugar

2 cups (480 mL) white wine vinegar

2 cups (480 mL) water

1 cup (50 g) Genovese or large-leaf basil, fresh and clean

8 cloves garlic, peeled

METHOD

Prepare the tomatoes according to standard canning procedure. In a large saucepan, heat 3 quarts (3 L) of water to a medium boil. Place the tomatoes in a basket, then lower them into the boiling water for 20 to 30 seconds, or until the skins begin to crack and split. Remove from the boiling water, and dip the basket of tomatoes in cold water for approximately 1 minute. Remove the basket from the cold water and set aside.

In a medium saucepan, heat the salt, sugar, vinegar, and water over medium heat until the liquid begins to bubble. Reduce the heat and keep the liquid hot. Core and peel the tomatoes. Pack them into hot, sterilized jars with the basil and garlic. Pour the hot vinegar water over the tomato mixture, leaving ½ inch (1.3 cm) of head room.

Depending on the volume of the tomatoes in the jar, you may need to adjust the amount of liquid. To do this, simply combine equal parts of vinegar and water to cover the tomatoes once they are packed. Release any air bubbles. Arrange the lids and adjust the caps. Process the jars in a hot-water bath for 30 minutes. Remove the jars and set aside to seal and cool before storing.

those ancient aromatics

Half the fun of pickling comes from the delicious smells that waft through the kitchen as you work. When pondering the pickle, remember the aromas that blend with it so well. Peppercorns, sage, mustard, caraway, and dill are but a few of the herbs and spices which infuse a unique twist of flavor and fancy into foods that would be less exotic by far. Some say Cleopatra fancied her pickles partly for their scent of cloves, while cooks on the isle of Mikinos perfumed their brined feta with oregano and basil.

TIERED ORANGES, TANGERINES, AND KUMQUATS

Wait for citrus season, then select the freshest produce for this festive combination. This recipe graces any poultry, rice, or stuffing with a slightly sweet and tangy flair. Or simply warm this mixture with a little honey, and serve it with pound cake or as a side to warm custard. If you plan to create food baskets for the holidays, be sure to include a jar of oranges!

YIELD: 4 pint (.5 L) jars
SHELF LIFE: Up to 6 months
PROCESSING METHOD: Hot pack; hot-water bath
HEAD SPACE: ½ inch (1.3 cm)
PROCESSING TIME: 10 minutes

INGREDIENTS

4–5 medium seedless oranges, sliced lengthwise and cleaned of membrane

4–5 clementines, or smaller seedless tangerines, sliced lengthwise and cleaned of membrane

20 (approximately) kumquats, whole and unpeeled

3 cinnamon sticks, each approximately 2–3 inches (5–7.5 cm) in length

12 whole cloves

2 cups (480 mL) white wine vinegar

4¼ cups (850 g) sugar

¾ cups (180 mL) water

METHOD

Place the oranges and tangerines in a medium saucepan. Add just enough water to cover the fruit. Pierce the skins of the kumquats and place them in a separate small saucepan, adding just enough water to cover them. To cook and tenderize the fruit, bring both saucepans to a medium boil, reduce the heat, then cover and steep for 25 to 30 minutes. Drain all of the fruit and set aside.

Place the cinnamon and cloves in a spice bag or large stainless steel tea ball. In a large saucepan, bring the vinegar, sugar, water, cinnamon, and cloves to a low boil. Add the drained fruit and simmer for 10 minutes. If you prefer a thicker juice, simmer longer. Remove the spice bag or tea ball.

Ladle the hot mixture into hot sterilized jars, allowing ½ inch (1.3 cm) of head room. Cover with the lids and adjust the caps. Process in a hot-water bath for 10 minutes. Remove the jars and set aside to seal and cool before storing.

JAMAICAN JERK SAUCE

Jerking is a Jamaican tradition that dates back more than 300 years. It is a way to put heat, spice, and tang in poultry, fish, or meat. If Jamaican dishes rub you the right way, you'll enjoy extending the ingredients into this sauce. The blend of chilies, garlic, and spices can be prepared in advance and successfully refrigerated for approximately one week. However, you can easily double or even triple this recipe for long-term storage, or for making gifts for a few treasured friends.

YIELD: 2 half-pint (.25 L) jars
SHELF LIFE: For the refrigerator, 7–10 days. With processing, up to 3 months
PROCESSING METHOD: Fresh for the refrigerator; or, hot pack; hot-water bath
HEAD SPACE: ½ inch (1.3 cm) for hot pack only
PROCESSING TIME: 20 minutes in a hot-water bath

INGREDIENTS

- 1 cup chopped scallions (180 g), white and green parts
- ½ cup (120 mL) lime juice
- ¾ cup (180 mL) apple cider vinegar
- ¼ cup (85 g) dark molasses
- ½ cup (120 mL) soy sauce
- ¼ cup (45 g) fresh ginger, chopped
- 6 cloves fresh garlic, chopped
- 2 jalapeño chilies, seeded and diced
- 2 serrano chilies, seeded and diced
- ½ teaspoon cinnamon, ground
- ½ teaspoon nutmeg, ground

METHOD

In a food processor or blender, place the scallions, lime juice, vinegar, molasses, soy sauce, ginger, garlic, chilies, cinnamon, and nutmeg. Pulse for approximately 10 seconds, until the ingredients are mixed but still a bit coarse. Transfer the mixture to a medium saucepan, and cook over medium heat until bubbly. Serve immediately, refrigerate, or process.

FOR THE REFRIGERATOR: Transfer the hot sauce immediately to a small container and allow the sauce to cool to room temperature. Cover and refrigerate.

FOR PROCESSING: Pour the hot sauce into hot, sterilized jars, leaving ½ inch (1.3 cm) of head room. Apply the lids, adjust caps, and process in a hot-water bath for 20 minutes. Remove jars, and allow to cool in a draft-free area before storing.

MUSTARD GREENS AND SCALLIONS

Soured mustard greens, cabbage, and alliums have long been used in Asian cuisine. This recipe is a combination of imagination and inspiration, fueled by conversation with a good friend. Hsaio Ching Chou's family uses pickled or soured greens in a number of stir-fry dishes at their restaurant in Missouri. When I told her about this cookbook, she said, "Oh, you must include a recipe for pickled greens—they're my favorite!" You will need a 1½ gallon (6 L) jar or crock for the brining process

YIELD: Approximately 3 pint (.5 L) jars

SHELF LIFE: Up to 2 weeks in the refrigerator

PROCESSING METHOD: Brining at room temperature

INGREDIENTS

    1 pound (448 g) mustard greens, cleaned and thoroughly dried, including chopped leaves and stems

    8 scallions, chopped, including white and green parts

 ½ cup (90 g) water chestnuts, sliced

    5 teaspoons pickling salt

    2 tablespoons wheat-free tamari sauce

1½ teaspoons sugar

    1 quart (1 L) water

METHOD

Toss the greens, scallions, and water chestnuts together in a large bowl, and set aside. Place the salt, tamari, sugar, and water in the jar or crock, and blend thoroughly with a whisk. Use a slotted spoon to transfer the greens mixture from the bowl to the crock. Gently press the greens under the brine a small batch at a time until all of the greens are submerged in the brine.

Cover the mixture with a dish or freezer bag filled with enough water to keep all of the ingredients under the surface. Be sure the dish or bag completely covers the surface. If necessary, weight the plate with a jar or glass filled with water to keep your greens beneath the brine.

Let the container stand at room temperature for 2 to 3 days. When the brining is completed, your greens should be sour, but mildly so. Transfer the greens to airtight jars, and refrigerate until ready to use.

PRESERVED GRAPE LEAVES

I lived at least a dozen summers beneath the leaves of our grape arbor, as the morning sun ushered in afternoons that heated, then glazed, bushels of purple, white, and red fruit. We watched and waited as hard little pea-sized beads grew to round and oval splendor. We ate fresh grapes, and made quarts of grape juice, but never gave a thought to the leaves. Years later, as I became acquainted with Middle Eastern cuisine, I came to appreciate what a grape leaf could do when wrapped around steaming rice blended with herbs and raisins. That's when I decided to take a little time to invest in preserving a pint or two for the pantry.

YIELD: Approximately 2 pint (.5 L) jars
SHELF LIFE: Up to 6 months
PROCESSING METHOD: Cold pack; hot-water bath
HEAD SPACE: ½ inch (1.3 cm)
PROCESSING TIME: 15 minutes

INGREDIENTS

2 tablespoons pickling salt

2 quarts (2 L) water

50–60 young, fresh grape leaves, free from spots or bruises

2½ cups (600 mL) water blended with 1 teaspoon citric acid

METHOD

Gently wash the grape leaves and pat dry. In a large pot, add the salt to the water, and bring to a boil over medium heat. Blanch the grape leaves for approximately 20 to 30 seconds, or until they are bright with color and still firm but pliant. Don't attempt to place all the leaves in the pot at the same time. It is better to work in smaller batches. Drain the leaves and set aside.

In another pot, bring the water and the citric acid to a simmer, then keep it hot over low heat. Stack the grape leaves several at a time, then fold or roll each stack, and gently pack into the hot jars. Depending on the number of leaves in each stack, you will be able to fit several stacks in each jar. Pour the hot citric-acid water over the leaves, gently pressing them down with a wooden spoon so they remain immersed in the brine while maintaining the proper head room. Release the air bubbles, apply the lids to the jars, and adjust the caps.

Process the jars in a hot-water bath for 15 minutes, remove the jars, and allow them to seal and cool to room temperature before storing.

If you wish to refrigerate this recipe for immediate use without processing, pack the grapes leaves with the brine in the hot jars, apply a nonreactive cap, and cool to room temperature before transferring to the refrigerator.

THOUSAND-YEAR-OLD EGGS

The term "thousand" or "hundred" refers to chicken or duck eggs traditionally preserved in a blend of salt, lime, and ashes. This technique dates back to the Ming Dynasty when raw eggs were placed in a bowl or pot, blanketed with the lime mixture, then buried in a shallow bed of dirt, and left to pickle for approximately 100 days. The lime petrified or hardened the eggs, while the salt preserved and shriveled them a bit.

The end result is an egg that looks like it's been buried for at least 100 years, with a slightly amber outer color, and a dark greenish yolk. These eggs were traditionally eaten uncooked, primarily because they were pretty firm when unearthed. The process is still employed today, and salted or dry preserved eggs come tidily wrapped and available in Asian markets.

This recipe is an adaptation that brines raw eggs for 45 days, and calls for eating them cooked once the preservation process is complete. While they don't follow Chinese tradition to the letter, try them as a side dish, or add them to your favorite stir fry. Note: the eggs can stay in the brine for more than 45 days if you prefer. However, you'll need to test them and adjust the brining time to your own taste. Be aware that they can become too salty if left for more than four to six weeks in the lime and salt solution.

YIELD: 12 eggs
SHELF LIFE: Use within 24 hours after cooking
PROCESSING METHOD: Brining in refrigerator
PROCESSING TIME: 45 days

INGREDIENTS
FOR THE BRINE

1¼ quarts (1.25 L) water

⅓ cup (65 g) pickling salt or coarse kosher salt

3 tablespoons pickling lime

12 chicken or duck eggs

FOR COOKING

Water for boiling

¼ cup (60 mL) soy sauce

2 scallions, trimmed of roots and green tips, and cut in half lengthwise.

METHOD

In a medium saucepan, bring the salt and water for the brine to a slow boil. Blend with a whisk until the salt has been completely dissolved. Remove the pan from the stove, and allow to cool to room temperature. Add the lime, blending it into the brine with a whisk. Set aside.

Place the eggs in a small enamel crock or jar. Pour the brine over the eggs, place a lid on the crock or jar, and refrigerate for 45 days.

When you are ready to use the eggs, place them in a small saucepan and cover them with cold water. Add the soy sauce and the scallions. Bring the water to a boil, lower the heat, and simmer the eggs for 15 minutes. Remove the pan from the stove, and plunge the eggs into cold water. Allow them to stand for 1 to 2 minutes, then rinse and apply a fresh batch of very cold water to the pan. Once the eggs are completely cold, drain and peel. Serve with radishes and greens as a side dish, or blend into a stir fry (see the recipe on page 103). Always use the eggs within 24 hours after cooking.

SUPER-CHUNKY COOKED SALSA

When we moved from New Jersey to Colorado in the late seventies, pickling and canning assumed a whole new dimension—CHILIES. Until that point in time, my knowledge of peppers remained fairly focused on bells, paprika, and sweeter varieties. As life in the west introduced jalapeños, fresh blue corn tortillas, chalupas, and more, I became intrigued by the process of making salsa. I hunted the farmers' markets for Anaheims, serranos, tomatillos, and the vast array of ingredients which harmonize so splendidly with southwestern fare. This recipe for cooked salsa has remained a household favorite for more than 20 years. Note: You will want to plan your time for a two-day recipe; you assemble the salsa, then allow it to cure overnight before processing.

INGREDIENTS

 20 poblano chilies, roasted, seeded, and peeled

  2 yellow bell peppers, seeded and chopped

  2 orange bell peppers, seeded and chopped

  6 serrano chilies, seeded and chopped

  1 large white onion, peeled and diced

  3 tablespoons ground cumin

1½ teaspoons ground cinnamon

  ½ teaspoon ground cayenne pepper

1½ teaspoons coarsely ground dried jalapeños

  2 cans crushed tomatoes in their juice,
     each can 28 ounces (784 g)

  1 tomato can filled with water
     (use one of the 28-ounce [784 g] cans)

  2 tablespoons light brown sugar

  2 tablespoons salt

  ⅓ cup (80 mL) cider vinegar

  1 cup (48 g) fresh cilantro, chopped

     Juice of 3 limes

YIELD: 6 pint (.5 L) jars
SHELF LIFE: 6 months for best flavor
PROCESSING METHOD: Hot pack; hot-water bath
HEAD SPACE: ½ inch (1.3 cm)
PROCESSING TIME: 15 minutes in a hot-water bath

METHOD

Chop the roasted peppers and set aside in a small bowl. Place the bell peppers, serranos, onion, cumin, cinnamon, cayenne, and jalapeños in a deep roaster or Dutch oven. Add the roasted poblanos, the crushed tomatoes, water, light brown sugar, salt, and vinegar. Stir the mixture in order to blend all of the ingredients, and cook over medium heat until the liquid reduces approximately 1 inch (2.5 cm). Remove the pan from the heat. Add the cilantro and lime juice, and blend well.

Allow the pan of salsa to cool to room temperature. Cover it with cheesecloth and refrigerate overnight. The next day, remove the pan from the refrigerator and cook the salsa over medium heat, stirring constantly, for 20 to 30 minutes. The salsa should be bubbly hot.

Spoon the hot salsa into hot, sterilized jars, leaving ½ inch (1.3 cm) of head room. Use a bubble freer to release any excess air from this very chunky mixture. Process for 15 minutes in a hot-water bath. Remove the jars, and set aside to cool in a draft-free area before storing.

NOTE: *Of course, you shouldn't feel compelled to process all of the cooked salsa for the pantry. Allow a jar or two to cool to room temperature, and serve immediately; or store in the refrigerator where it will keep up to 10 days—if it lasts that long!*

YIELD: 2 pint (.5 L) jars
SHELF LIFE: In the refrigerator for up to 1 week
PROCESSING METHOD: Cold pack refrigerator pickle
HEAD SPACE: ½ inch (1.3 cm)
PROCESSING TIME: None

INGREDIENTS

30–40 fresh asparagus spears

½ cup (120 mL) white balsamic vinegar

½ cup (120 mL) white wine vinegar

½–¾ cup (120–180 mL) water

1 teaspoon granulated sugar

½ teaspoon kosher salt per pint

3–4 leaves of lemon verbena, or ½ teaspoon of dried verbena per jar

METHOD

Rinse the asparagus and trim off the bottom ends, leaving spears each approximately 3½ inches (8.8 cm) in length. (You will be standing them on end in the jars with the tips pointing up.) Place the asparagus in a colander to drain.

In a small saucepan, bring the vinegars, water, sugar, and salt to a boil over medium heat. Reduce the heat and simmer for another 2 minutes. Remove the pan from the heat, partially cover, and allow to cool slightly while you are packing the asparagus.

Place the asparagus in hot, sterilized jars, with the tip of the spear pointing upward. As you pack, add the lemon verbena, either fresh or dried. Pour the warm vinegar liquid into the jars, allowing ½ inch (1.3 m) of head room, and release any excess air with a bubble freer. Apply the lids, adjust the caps, and allow the pints to cool completely before placing in the refrigerator for 48 hours before using.

ASPARAGUS WITH LEMON VERBENA

Asparagus, in my opinion, are really best when steamed or broiled for about five minutes before serving. I find that traditional canning procedures tend to cause a quick dissipation of color as well as flavor. So, this recipe calls for creating the asparagus "pickle," which really marinates the spears in the refrigerator. The color and flavor stay fresher.

CARROT MEDLEY

Carrots, lemon thyme, and less than 20 minutes in the kitchen will add a grace note of color to your table and nutrition for your guests. This recipe has been dubbed a medley, since the vegetables can be arranged in any size and order for the jar you choose. Layer whole baby carrots against layers of slices, or simply stand them on end row upon row for visual interest. Pack them into a wide-mouth decorator jar, and you'll be able to take the jar straight from the refrigerator to the table.

YIELD: 2 pint (.5 L) jars, or 1 quart (1 L) jar according to carrot size

SHELF LIFE: Up to 2 weeks in the refrigerator

PROCESSING METHOD: Refrigerator pickle

HEAD SPACE: 1/2 inch (1.3 cm)

PROCESSING TIME: None required

INGREDIENTS

1 pound (.45 kg) carrots, either sliced, whole, or in spears

1 clove garlic, chopped

1 teaspoon pickling salt

4 sprigs of fresh lemon thyme, approximately 3 inches long (7.5 cm)

1 pinch lemon zest

1/4 cup (36 g) light brown sugar

1 cup (240 mL) white wine vinegar

1/2 cup (120 mL) orange juice

1/2 cup (120 mL) water

METHOD

In a medium saucepan, bring 1 quart (1 L) of water to a medium boil and blanch the carrots for 2 minutes. Remove the pot from the stove, and drain the carrots before plunging them into cold water. Drain again, and set aside. Allow the carrots to cool for approximately 5 minutes.

In a saucepan, bring the garlic, salt, thyme, lemon zest, brown sugar, white wine vinegar, orange juice, and water to a low boil. Reduce the heat under the pan, keeping the liquid hot while packing the carrots. Pack or arrange the carrots in hot jars. Ladle the hot liquid over the carrots, leaving 1/2 inch (1.3 cm) head room. Apply the lids to the jars, and adjust the caps. Allow the carrots to cool to room temperature. Refrigerate for 24 hours before serving.

EGGPLANT WITH MINT

If you are a kitchen gardener who cultivates eggplant, you know that its development provides a unique tint to your vegetable patch. Be it white, purple, or the speckled heirloom variety, eggplant gathers color with a glow as the summer progresses. This recipe for pickled eggplant is a favorite regardless of the season. It reflects a distinctly Greek and southern Italian preference for fresh mint in the kitchen. Allow it to steep for two to three days before serving.

YIELD: 1 wide-mouth quart (1 L) jar
SHELF LIFE: Up to 3 weeks in the refrigerator
PROCESSING METHOD: Marinated refrigerator pickle
HEAD SPACE: 1/2 inch (1.3 cm)
PROCESSING: None

INGREDIENTS

    1   medium eggplant, peeled and
        sliced to 1/8 inch (.3 cm) thickness

    1   cup (240 mL) white balsamic vinegar

 1/4   cup (60 mL) white distilled vinegar

    1   cup (240 mL) water

    1   teaspoon granulated sugar

 1/4   teaspoon kosher salt

 1/2   teaspoon freshly ground black pepper

    3   cloves of garlic, peeled and minced

    2   tablespoons extra virgin olive oil

10–15 leaves of fresh mint (or to taste)

METHOD

Place the peeled and sliced eggplant in a large bowl filled with 2 quarts (2 L) of water. Cover, allow the eggplant to soak 1 hour, then drain in a colander. Squeeze out any excess water.

In a small saucepan, blend the vinegars, water, sugar, salt, pepper, and garlic. Bring to a boil, then lower the heat, and simmer for 5 minutes. Remove the pan from the heat, blend in the olive oil with a whisk, and set aside.

Place the eggplant and a few mint leaves in the bottom of the jar, then continue to layer the eggplant and mint to the top, leaving 1/2 inch (1.3 cm) of head room.

Pour the liquid over the eggplant, and release any excess air with a bubble freer. Apply the lid, adjust the cap, and allow the jar to cool completely before refrigerating. Your eggplant tastes best when it has been allowed to steep for 2 to 3 days before use.

RED FLANNEL PICKLES

Good friend and colleague Cathy Morrison shared this recipe with me. It came from her mother, Mildred Morrison, who got the recipe from her friend Nancy Woodall from Greenville, Texas. Nancy's mother, Nan Hart began the whole relay some years ago, when this recipe for "red flannels" became a tradition in her kitchen. It all leads me to believe that pickles and friends can create heartwarming legacies. If you are making the Classic Dills on page 84, use a few to create this colorful, pickled-cucumber variation.

INGREDIENTS

2 cups (400 g) granulated sugar

1 cup (240 mL) cider vinegar

12 dill pickles, cut crosswise in ¼-inch-thick (.6 cm) slices

⅓ cup (60 g) canned pimento strips

METHOD

In a small saucepan, blend the sugar and vinegar. Cook over medium heat, stirring constantly. Add the pickle slices and pimento strips, and bring the mixture to a boil over medium heat.

Spoon the pickles, pimentos, and juice into hot, sterilized jars. Apply the lids, adjust the caps, and allow to cool to room temperature in a draft-free area. Transfer to the refrigerator.

NOTE: *I've found that this recipe tastes best when the pickles have been allowed to sit for a week before serving.*

YIELD: 2 pint (.5 L) jars
SHELF LIFE: 4–6 weeks in the refrigerator
PROCESSING METHOD: Hot pack
HEAD SPACE: ½ inch (1.3 cm)
PROCESSING TIME: None

ALMOND-STUFFED JALAPEÑOS WITH OPAL BASIL

While some pickled peppers are created for use in making sauces, soups, and main dishes, these jalapeños simply need to be consumed for their own merit. The blend of almond sweetness with chili heat creates a flavor some call habit forming. Regardless, they are easy to process, and a surefire way to take advantage of the harvest!

INGREDIENTS

25–30	jalapeños chilies
25–30	whole almonds, blanched
½	teaspoon kosher salt for each pint (.5 L)
6	cloves garlic, peeled
6	large leaves of opal or purple-ruffle basil
6–8	cups (1.5–1.9 L) white distilled vinegar, boiling hot

METHOD

Cut the outer stems from the jalapeños, rinse, and pat dry. Slit the skin of each jalapeño with the tip of a sharp knife. Place one almond into each slit in each jalapeño and set aside.

Spoon the salt into the bottoms of the pint jars. Add the garlic and the basil. Pack the peppers into the jars. Pour the boiling hot vinegar over the peppers, allowing ½ inch (1.3 cm) head room, and release any excess air with a bubble freer. Apply the lids, adjust the caps, and process for 10 minutes in a hot-water bath. Remove the jars and set aside to cool in a draft-free area before storing.

YIELD: 6 pint (.5 L) jars
SHELF LIFE: 6 MONTHS
PROCESSING METHOD: Cold pack; hot-water bath
HEAD SPACE: ½ inch (1.3 cm)
PROCESSING TIME: 15 minutes in a hot-water bath

SAUERKRAUT

The Chinese may not have discovered sauerkraut as we know it, but they certainly contributed to the chain of culinary events that allows us to continue to enjoy this food today. Much more than a topping for frankfurters, sauerkraut nourishes our bodies and fortifies our souls. It provides a strong source of vitamin C and beneficial lactic acid to our diets. With a few pounds of cabbage, and a modicum of salt, you can be on your way to a healthy addition for the dinner table as well as the pantry. This recipe calls for 15 pounds (6.7 kg) of cabbage. The number of heads you use will depend on their size.

YIELD: Approximately 5–6 quart (1 L) jars of sauerkraut

SHELF LIFE: 12 months

PROCESSING METHOD: Brining; hot pack; hot-water bath

HEAD SPACE: ½ inch (1.3 cm)

PROCESSING TIME: 20 minutes in a hot-water bath

INGREDIENTS

15 pounds (6.7 kg) winter cabbage

10 tablespoons kosher salt

METHOD

Purchase or harvest perfectly fresh cabbage, and allow the heads to sit for a day in your kitchen. Remove the outer leaves, rinse all of the heads, and allow them to drain for 15 to 20 minutes. First cut the cabbage heads in half from top to bottom, then horizontally, until all of the cabbage is quartered. Using a food processor or vegetable shredder, cut the quarters into thin shreds, less than ⅛ inch (.3 cm) thick.

In a large glass bowl or container, blend approximately 5 to 6 pounds (2.2 to 2.7 kg) of the cabbage with 4 tablespoons of the salt. Allow the cabbage to stand for 15 to 20 minutes, or until it begins to wilt. (This process softens the cabbage a little, which allows for less damage to the individual shreds as you pack them in the crock.)

Transfer the wilted cabbage to a large, clean earthenware crock. Using your hands, gently press down on the cabbage until juice begins to come to the surface. Continue the process of salting, wilting, and packing the cabbage, until you have used it all, or have packed the crock to within 4 to 5 inches (10 to 12.5 cm) from the top.

Cover the cabbage with a clean muslin cloth or a piece of plastic wrap. Tuck the ends of the material down into the sides of the crock. Cover the material with a plate that just fits inside the diameter of the crock. Use a covered jar or plastic bag filled with water to weigh the plate (and cabbage) down, causing the brine to rise just enough to meet the edge of the plate, but not cover its surface. (You may need to adjust the amount of water in the jar or bag until you find the right weight to achieve the desired level.)

Allow the crock of cabbage to rest at a temperature of 68 to 72°F (20 to 25°C) for best results. Too low a temperature will prevent sufficient fermentation, while too much heat can speed up the process and cause spoilage. You should have sauerkraut in 5 to 6 weeks.

To process the sauerkraut once it's fermented, transfer the sauerkraut and its juice to a large pot or Dutch oven, and heat until the temperature in the kraut reaches 185 to 210°F (82 to 99°C). Be sure that you heat, not boil, the sauerkraut.

Ladle the sauerkraut into hot, sterilized jars, leaving ½ inch (1.3 cm) of head room. Apply the lids, adjust the caps, and process in a hot water bath for 20 minutes. Remove the jars, and set aside to cool in a draft-free area before storing.

SPICED WHOLE ONIONS

Pickled onions lend a memory of summer to those months that carry a bit of chill in the air. And regardless of color, either red, yellow, or white, they offer a spicy redolence to any main dish, salad, or condiment platter. Onions rank at the top of the vegetable list for retained nutrition and flavor when pickled, and they make perfect candidates for long-term storage. Onions are "good keepers."

This recipe calls for placing the onions in their jars to create layers of yellow, white, and red. However, you can also mix all of the onions together for an equally pleasing visual affect.

INGREDIENTS

- 1 pound (448 g) each yellow, red, and white boiling onions
- 1½ cups (360 mL) white distilled vinegar
- 1 cup (240 mL) water
- 1 tablespoon light brown sugar
- 1 teaspoon kosher salt
- 1 tablespoon mixed pickling spice
- ¼ teaspoon ground ginger

YIELD: 2 pint (.5 L) jars
SHELF LIFE: 12 months
PROCESSING METHOD: Hot pack; hot-water bath
HEAD SPACE: ½ inch (1.3 cm)
PROCESSING TIME: 15 minutes in a hot-water bath

METHOD

Cut a thin slice from the stem and root ends of the onions. Rub or peel off any outer papery skin. Bring approximately 1 quart (1 L) of water to a boil in a medium saucepan. Blanch the yellow onions. Remove from the pan, and allow to cool for 5 minutes before rinsing under cool water. Transfer the onions to a colander, and set aside to drain. Follow this procedure for the red then the white onions.

In a medium saucepan, blend the vinegar, water, sugar, salt, pickling spice, and ginger. Bring the ingredients to a boil over medium heat, then reduce the heat and allow the liquid to simmer for 5 minutes.

Place the onions in hot sterilized jars in layers of yellow, white, and red, leaving ½ inch (1.3 cm) of head room. Pour the hot liquid over the onions, and release any excess air with a bubble freer. Apply the lids, adjust the caps, and process for 15 minutes in a hot-water bath. Remove the jars and set aside to cool in a draft-free area before storing.

CLASSIC SWEETS

This recipe came to me from my mother's kitchen more than 20 years ago. I always enjoy reading through this recipe because of the handwritten editorial note at the end of it, "Amen and good luck!" Although not much is needed with this recipe, my mother's opinion has added a sense of adventure—which is probably why I enjoy creating new recipes to this day.

YIELD: Approximately 6 pint (.5 L) jars

SHELF LIFE: 6 months

PROCESSING METHOD: Hot pack; hot-water bath

HEAD SPACE: ½ inch (1.3 cm)

PROCESSING TIME: 10 minutes

INGREDIENTS

- 20 cucumbers, each approximately 4 inches (10 cm) long, cut into slices
- 3 large, sweet onions, diced
- ⅓ cup (67 g) salt
- 3 cups (720 mL) cider vinegar
- 5 cups (1 kg) sugar
- 1½ teaspoons turmeric
- 2 tablespoons mustard seed
- 1½ teaspoons celery seed
- 2 tablespoons pickling spice

METHOD

Place the cucumbers in a large enamel or nonreactive pot. Toss in the onions and the salt. Cover with ice cubes and let stand for 3 hours. Drain thoroughly and set aside. Prepare the brine. In a large saucepan, bring the vinegar, sugar, turmeric, mustard seed, celery seed, and pickling spice to a boil. Add the cucumber slices, and blend all of the ingredients. Bring the mixture back to a boil, and allow it to bubble for 5 minutes. Pack the hot mixture into hot, sterilized jars, allowing ½ inch (1.3 m) of head room. Release any air bubbles. Apply the lids, adjust the caps, and process for 10 minutes in a hot-water bath. Remove the jars from the bath and set aside to cool. Amen. And *good luck*!

BALSAMIC CIPOLLINI

Cipollini means "little button" in Italian. When you look at cipollini onions, it's evident how they got their name. These sweet, flat renditions of the allium family have been charming Italian palates for centuries. Cipollini are available from late summer through December, and can be found in most well-stocked grocery stores, usually in the specialty produce section.

Don't purchase these from the supermarket unless you can find out when they were harvested and shipped. As with all pickling produce, freshness counts. But with cipollini, you want to capture them at the peak of their sweetness. This recipe is meant for processing, but you can halve the recipe and make a batch for the refrigerator, where your onions will retain their flavor and crunch for up to three weeks.

YIELD: 2 quart (1 L) jars
SHELF LIFE: For the refrigerator, 3 weeks. With processing, up to 3 months
PROCESSING METHOD: Hot pack; hot-water bath
HEAD SPACE: ½ inch (1.3 cm)
PROCESSING TIME: 15 minutes in a hot-water bath

INGREDIENTS

1 quart (1 L) white wine vinegar
2½ cups (600 mL) water
¼ cup (60 mL) extra virgin olive oil
3 cloves garlic, peeled and sliced (If you can find or grow rocambole, it's the best for this recipe.)
1 tablespoon kosher salt
¼ cup (35 g) light brown sugar, loosely packed
½ teaspoon black pepper, coarsely ground
6 fresh leaves of sweet basil
40 cipollini onions
½ cup (120 mL) balsamic vinegar

METHOD

Combine the white wine vinegar, water, olive oil, garlic, salt, sugar, black pepper, and basil in a medium saucepan. Stir with a whisk, and bring the ingredients to a boil. Remove from the heat, partially cover, and set aside.

Cut any excess stems away from the onions, and make a crosscut at the stem end. Drop the onions into a pot of boiling water, and cook for 5 to 7 minutes, or until the onions start to change color. Remove the pot from the heat, and allow it to stand for 5 minutes. Drain the onions and rinse them with cold water. When they are cool enough to handle, use your fingertips to rub away the outer skins. Skin all the onions.

Return the pot of seasoned vinegar to the heat and bring to a simmer. Add the onions and cook for another 3 to 4 minutes. Gently lift the onions out of the pot and into hot, sterilized jars. Add the balsamic vinegar to the seasoned vinegar, blend with a whisk, and immediately pour the hot liquid over the onions, leaving ½ inch (1.3 cm) of head room. Release any excess air with a bubble freer. Apply the lids, adjust the caps, and process for 15 minutes in a hot-water bath. Remove the jars and allow them to sit in a draft-free area before storing.

NOTE: *If you plan to use your onions immediately, place them in the jars, add the balsamic vinegar mixture, apply the lids, and simply let the onions rest until completely cool. Then add and adjust the caps, and refrigerate for 3 days before using.*

CLASSIC DILLS

Brined or cured cucumbers remain one of the oldest, most favored pickles. From Cleopatra to Thomas Jefferson and America's Mr. Heinz, pickles, especially the salty dill variety, hold their own among other comfort foods. As June yawns open to the summer sky, look for fresh pickling cucumbers at your local market. Take a few home and brine your first batch. You'll be pleasantly surprised to learn that they are easy to make. Brined pickles may take a few weeks to cure, but you'll have little work to do while nature takes its course.

This recipe requires a 3-gallon (11.5 L) jar or crock. It will provide enough room for your pickles, as well as head room for the additional liquid that will be drawn out of the cucumbers as they ferment in the brine.

YIELD: 5 pounds (2.25 kg) of classic dills

SHELF LIFE: For the refrigerator, 3–4 weeks. With processing, up to 6 months

PROCESSING METHOD: Brining for long- or short-term storage. For the pantry, cold pack; hot-water bath

HEAD SPACE: ½ inch (1.3 cm)

PROCESSING TIME: When using quart (1 L) jars, 15 minutes in a hot-water bath; when using pint (.5 L) jars, 10 minutes in a hot-water bath

HERE ARE A FEW TIPS FOR BRINED PICKLES:

- Always use clean stone or glass crocks and jars

- Only use pickling varieties of cucumbers

- Always use pickling or Kosher salt, never use iodized salt

- Do not use hard water

INGREDIENTS

40	cucumber pickles, approximately 5 pounds (2.25 kg)
10–12	fresh grape leaves (optional)
5–6	bunches fresh dill
4	tablespoons whole pickling spices
1½	cups (300 g) kosher salt
2	cups (480 mL) white distilled vinegar
2	gallons (7.6 L) water

METHOD

Gently wash the cucumbers and inspect for nicks and bruises, discarding any damaged produce. Remove the stems and blossoms from the ends. Place the cucumbers in a colander and allow to drain for 5 to 10 minutes.

You will layer the ingredients in the crock. If you are using grape leaves, place 3 to 4 leaves and a small handful of dill in the bottom of the crock. If you are not using grape leaves, begin your layering with a small handful of dill. Next add the cucumbers until the layer is approximately ½-inch (1.3 cm) deep, then add a little spice mixture to this layer. Continue to layer the grape leaves (if you are using them), dill, cucumbers, and spice mixture until you end with a top layer of fresh dill.

Mix the salt, vinegar, and water together, and pour the solution over the cucumbers. Keep the leaves, dill, and cucumbers immersed by weighing them down with a plate topped by a covered jar full of water. (The weight of the jar should be just enough to barely cover the plate with the salt brine.) You can also use a plastic bag filled with water. Be sure the cucumbers remain immersed during the brining process; otherwise, airborne bacteria will cause fermentation of the wrong type, and your batch will grow harmful bacteria.

Cover the crock with a towel, and allow it to stand on a flat surface or an accessible shelf in your pantry. A consistent temperature of approximately 70°F (21°C) is best for brining.

After approximately 3 to 4 days, a layer of scum will begin to form on the surface of the liquid. Remove the scum with a shallow spoon, and continue to check the surface daily, removing scum as needed.

Allow the cucumbers to ferment for 3 to 4 weeks. At this point, your pickles are ready to rinse and eat, keep in the refrigerator, or process for future use

Pour the pickles and the brine into a colander that rests on a large nonreactive pot. Remove the colander and place it in the sink. Place the pot with the brine on the stove, and bring the brine to a boil. Reduce the heat and allow the brine to simmer for 5 minutes. Rinse the pickles under cold water, and set aside to drain well. (This is a good time to test the batch, and snatch your first taste of freshly cured pickle.)

If you want to prepare a few jars for the refrigerator, allow the brine to cool while packing the pickles into sterilized jars. Leaving ½ inch (1.3 cm) of head room, pour the brine over the pickles, then release any excess air with a bubble freer. Cap the jars and refrigerate where your pickles will retain good flavor and color for up to 3 to 4 weeks.

To process for the pantry, pack the pickles in hot sterilized jars. Pour the hot brine over the pickles, and release any excess air with a bubble freer. Apply the lids, adjust the caps, and process in a hot-water bath for 10 minutes if using pint (.5 L) jars, or for 15 minutes if using quart (1 L) jars. Remove the jars, and set them aside to cool in a draft-free area before storing.

SAPA!

In Italy, sapa probably came about as a response to an excess of grapes that were not quite right for making wine. Used as a dessert sauce, it frequently found its role atop mellow custards, poached pears, or pastries. Even today, its syrupy texture and tangy-sweet flavor make it the perfect foil for an after-dinner treat. In fact, some believe that sapa actually mothered the vinegar we know today as balsamic.

Sapa is light, full of flavor, and well worth the wait as crushed grapes steep in their own juice. You'll want to make sapa two to three days in advance of serving. Serve it chilled or warm with flan, waffles, or as a light sauce over fresh fruit and Bel Paese—when in doubt, make dessert!

This recipe doubles easily, and can be stored in the refrigerator or processed for the pantry. Be sure to look for plump, sweet grapes at the farmers' market or nearby orchard. Supermarket fare won't do!

YIELD: 2 pint (.5 L) jars
SHELF LIFE: For the refrigerator, up to 4 weeks. With processing, up to 3 months
PROCESSING METHOD: Hot pack; hot-water bath
HEAD SPACE: ½ inch (1.3 cm)
PROCESSING TIME: 15 minutes in a hot-water bath

INGREDIENTS

10 pounds (4.5 kg) fresh red grapes, such as Muscadine, Red Emperor, or Concord

1½ cups (360 mL) dry red table wine

2 tablespoons granulated sugar

METHOD

Rinse and remove the grapes from their stems. Be sure to look for and discard any damaged fruit. Place the grapes in a food processor, and process in batches until all of the fruit is finely chopped.

Transfer the grapes to a large glass bowl, cover, and refrigerate for 3 days. Pour the grapes through a strainer that rests above a large saucepan. Use your hands or a wooden spoon to press as much of the juice out of the fruit as possible.

Bring the grape juice to a boil over medium heat and cook for 20 minutes, or until it begins to thicken into a syrup. Stir in the wine and the sugar, and simmer for another 5 minutes.

To process for the pantry, pour the syrup into hot, sterilized jars, leaving ½ inch (1.3 cm) of head room. Apply the lids, adjust the caps, and process for 15 minutes in a hot-water bath. Remove th jars and set aside to cool in a draft-free area before storing.

To store in the refrigerator, pour the syrup into hot, sterilized jars, then set them aside to cool completely. Apply the lids and caps, and refrigerate for 2 to 3 days before serving.

YIELD: 2 pint (.5 L) jars

SHELF LIFE: With processing, up to 3 months. For the refrigerator, 5–7 days

PROCESSING METHOD: Cold pack; hot-water bath

HEAD SPACE: 1/2 inch (1.3 cm)

PROCESSING TIME: 10 minutes in a hot-water bath

INGREDIENTS

- 4 cups or approximately 1 pound (448 g) of fresh rhubarb, peeled and chopped into 1-inch (2.5 cm) pieces
- 2–3 Angelica leaves, cut into pieces
- 1 cup (240 mL) white distilled vinegar
- 1 cup (240 mL) water
- 1/2 teaspoon salt
- 2 tablespoons sugar
- 1 tablespoon fresh lemon juice

METHOD

In a small saucepan, blend the vinegar, water, salt, and sugar. Bring the liquid to a boil, reduce the heat, add the lemon juice, and simmer for 5 minutes.

Loosely pack the rhubarb and the Angelica into hot, sterilized jars. Pour the hot liquid over the fruit, allowing 1/2 inch (1.3 cm) of head room. Use a bubble freer to release any excess air, and process. Apply the lids, adjust the caps, and process for 10 minutes in a hot-water bath. Remove the jars and set aside to cool in a draft-free area before storing.

For the refrigerator, pack the jars, pour in the liquid, apply the lids and caps. Allow the jars to cool completely before transferring to the refrigerator where they will keep for 5 to 7 days.

RHUBARB ANGELICA

Angelica oficinalis is a native herb of northern Europe, prized throughout history for its culinary and medicinal properties. Our ancestors used the entire plant, eating the stalks like celery, and using the leaves to make wine, candy, and tonics for coughs and colds. Today, Angelica still resides in a position of honor by adding an accent of spice to rhubarb, enhancing its flavor for pies, cobblers, and custard sauce. This recipe is easy to process, allowing you to get in and out of the kitchen in less than an hour.

GINGER PEARS

Home-canned pickled pears have always been a favorite of mine. I think it's because they fill the kitchen with a blend of sweetness and spice as they make their way to the canner. Serve these chilled along with a few toasted almonds and a bloomy round of brie, or heat them to accompany grilled poultry or meats.

YIELD: Approximately 4 quart (1 L) jars
SHELF LIFE: 12 months
PROCESSING METHOD: Hot pack; hot-water bath
HEAD SPACE: ½ inch (1.3 cm)
PROCESSING TIME: 15 minutes in a hot-water bath

INGREDIENTS

5 pounds (2.24 kg) yellow or red Bartlett pears

3 cups (600 g) granulated sugar

4 cups (960 mL) water

2½ cups (600 mL) ginger brandy

1 tablespoon ground ginger

Juice from 2 lemons

2–3 orange slices for each jar (optional)

METHOD

Stem, peel, and halve the pears. Note: Pears, along with apples, peaches, and other fruits, tend to discolor once they're cut and waiting for processing. Once you've removed the stems and peeled the pears, gently place them in a solution of 1 gallon (3.8 L) of water, mixed with 2 tablespoons of vinegar and 2 tablespoons of salt. Allow the pears to sit for 10 minutes, then transfer them to a colander. Rinse them gently and set them aside to drain while you prepare the ginger syrup.

In a large saucepan, blend the sugar, water, brandy, ginger, and lemon juice with a whisk. Bring the ingredients to a boil, then reduce the heat. Transfer enough pear halves to the syrup in the saucepan so that they form a single layer, and cook for 5 minutes. Then, using a slotted spoon, transfer that batch of pears to hot, sterilized jars. Follow this procedure until all of the pears have been cooked and packed. Option: If you wish to add orange slices, place them in the bottom of the jars as you pack the pears.

Use a mesh strainer to strain the hot liquid as you pour it into the jars, leaving ½ inch (1.3 cm) of head room. Release any excess air with a bubble freer. Apply the lids, adjust the caps, and process for 15 minutes in a hot-water bath. Remove the jars and set aside to cool in a draft-free area before storing.

PINEAPPLE SALSA

Grace it with blue or yellow corn chips, add it to your next batch of enchiladas, or brush it onto vegetables for the grill. This multipurpose salsa gets its kick from fresh pineapple and pineapple vinegar (see recipe on page 41). You can prepare this recipe with today as well as tomorrow in mind—keep a jar in the refrigerator, and process an additional batch for the holidays.

YIELD:
Approximately
2 pint (.5 L) jars

SHELF LIFE:
6 months

PROCESSING METHOD: Hot pack; hot-water bath

HEAD SPACE:
½ inch (1.3 cm)

PROCESSING TIME:
15 minutes in a hot-water bath

INGREDIENTS

2 cups (360 g) coarsely chopped pineapple

1 cup (224 g) plum tomatoes, peeled, chopped, and seeded

2 jalapeño peppers, chopped, seeded, and deveined

¼ cup (36 g) light brown sugar

⅓ cup (80 mL) pineapple vinegar

2 tablespoons white distilled vinegar

1 teaspoon salt

½ teaspoon white pepper

METHOD

Combine all of the ingredients in a large bowl, cover, and refrigerate for 3 hours. To serve, remove from the refrigerator and bring to room temperature.

To process this recipe for future use, combine the ingredients in a medium saucepan and bring to a low boil. Allow the mixture to bubble for 5 minutes. Pack the hot mixture into hot jars, leaving ½ inch (1.3 cm) of head room. Apply the lids and adjust the caps. Process for 15 minutes in a hot-water bath. Remove, and set aside to cool in a draft-free area before storing.

BALSAMIC STRAWBERRIES

Strawberries are their most flavorful when they are consumed immediately after their release from the vine. Yet they lend a special addition to rhubarb pie, and infuse shortcake with a cause for celebration. Although most frequently paired with a little sugar, this fruit brings it own sweetness forward when blended with a little salt, pepper, and balsamic vinegar. Strawberries tend to lose color and flavor when processed, but this refrigerator recipe keeps the freshness for several days after preparation. You can make a batch of fresh sliced strawberries for immediate use (see the recipe for Mascarpone Filled Crepes on page 116), or pack them whole for future use.

INGREDIENTS

2 1/2 pounds (1.1 kg) fresh small strawberries

1/2 teaspoon salt

1/4 teaspoon finely ground black pepper

1/3 cup (65 g) white sugar

1 cup (240 mL) balsamic vinegar, imported and aged

METHOD

For immediate use, place the berries in a medium glass bowl. Add the salt, pepper, and sugar, and toss gently to coat the strawberries. Set the berries aside for 15 minutes. Add the balsamic vinegar. Cover and refrigerate until ready to use.

For future use, place whole strawberries in a medium bowl, and gently toss with the salt, pepper, and sugar. Set aside for 30 minutes. Use a slotted spoon to gently lift the strawberries out of the bowl and into the pint jars. Blend the balsamic vinegar with the berry juice left in the bowl. Pour over the fruit in the jars. Apply the lids, adjust the caps, and refrigerate until ready to use.

YIELD: 2 pint (.5 L) jars
SHELF LIFE: 3–5 days in the refrigerator
PROCESSING METHOD: Cold pack
HEAD SPACE: 1/2 inch (1.3 cm)
PROCESSING TIME: None

YIELD: 1 quart (1 L) jar; or 2 pint (.5 L) jars
SHELF LIFE: Up to 6 months
PROCESSING METHOD: Cold pack; hot-water bath
HEAD SPACE: ½ inch (1.3 cm)
PROCESSING TIME: 20 minutes in a hot-water bath

INGREDIENTS

2 large, smooth-skinned lemons

3 medium, smooth-skinned navel oranges

2 cups (480 mL) white balsamic vinegar

½ cup (120 mL) water

3 cups (600 g) granulated sugar

¼ teaspoon kosher salt

4 whole cloves

METHOD

Select perfect lemons and oranges, wash, then pat them dry. Use a sharp knife to cut a slice from the stem and blossom ends of all of the fruit. Then cut the lemons crosswise into slices, each ⅛ inch (.3 cm) thick. Remove the seeds from the slices with the tip of a paring knife, and set the slices aside in a small bowl. Follow the same procedure for the oranges.

In a medium saucepan, blend the vinegar, water, sugar, and salt. Bring the ingredients to a boil, reduce the heat, and simmer for 5 minutes.

Place 4 cloves in the bottom of a hot, sterilized jar if processing a quart (1 L) jar, or 2 cloves in each jar if processing 2 pint (.5 L) jars. Add the lemons and oranges, alternating them in layers. Pour the hot liquid over the fruit, allowing ½ inch (1.3 cm) of head room. Release any excess air with a bubble freer. Apply the lids, adjust the caps, and process in a hot-water bath for 20 minutes. Remove the jar or jars and set aside to cool in a draft-free area before storing.

SWEET LEMONS AND ORANGES

As September sun yields to the first snows of winter, harvest bounty fades for most home-grown produce. While vegetables such as potatoes, cabbage, apples, and carrots remain good candidates for long-term storage, fresh home-grown fruit disappears until the next season. However, that urge to pickle doesn't stop even though the peaches disappear! When lemons, oranges, and other citrus fruits come into season, I search the local markets for the freshest I can find. Pickling lemons with oranges offers versatility to a variety of foods, from baked ham to a warm fruit compote.

CHERRY TORTE

This combination of Queen Anne and dark Bing cherries creates a stunning effect, as the yellow and dark red fruit gets layered along with almonds for visual appeal. While this recipe requires a bit of advance planning, you'll be rewarded with a fruit torte that stands well in "decorator" quart (1 L) or half-gallon (2 L) jars.

YIELD: 2 quart (1 L) jars, or 1 half-gallon (2 L) jar
SHELF LIFE: 12 months
PROCESSING METHOD: Steeped; cold pack; hot-water bath
HEAD SPACE: 1/2 inch (1.3 cm)
PROCESSING TIME: 15 minutes in a hot-water bath

INGREDIENTS

3 cups (504 g) Bing cherries, cleaned, stemmed, pitted, and pierced

3 cups (504 g) Queen Anne cherries, cleaned, stemmed, pitted, and pierced

2 cups (480 mL) white balsamic vinegar

2 cups (480 mL) water

2 cardamom pods

1 teaspoon vanilla extract, good quality

1/2 teaspoon almond extract

2 1/2 cups (500 g) granulated sugar

1 cup (85 g) whole blanched almonds

METHOD

Place the Queen Anne cherries in one bowl and the Bing cherries in another separate bowl. In a medium saucepan, blend the vinegar, water, cardamom, vanilla, almond extract, and sugar. Bring the ingredients to a boil, reduce the heat, and simmer for 10 minutes. Remove the pan from the heat, and set aside for 20 minutes to cool.

Pour equal amounts of the cooled mixture into each bowl of cherries, cover the bowls, and allow them to steep overnight. The next day, drain the juice from both bowls of fruit and transfer to one medium saucepan. Heat the liquid over medium heat until it begins to bubble, then remove the pan from the heat and set aside.

Spoon the cherries into hot, sterilized jars, creating layers from the two colors as you would for a torte. Place a layer of almonds between each layer of cherries. Pour the liquid over the fruit and nuts, leaving 1/2 inch (1.3 cm) of head room. Use a bubble freer to release any excess air. Apply the lids, adjust the caps, and process for 15 minutes in a hot-water bath. Remove the jars and place in a draft-free area to cool before storing, Allow the cherries to cure for 3 weeks before serving

SPICED ITALIAN PLUMS

My parents loved to garden and watch their fruit trees grow. Although our plot in Pennsylvania measured just about a half-acre, they managed to have enough room to raise their children, along with chickens, gardens, grapes, apples, pears, cherries, and plums. I can remember watching my father prune the plum trees, check the blossoms, and talk about the harvest. We raised green and red plums for eating, but the purple (and prolific) Italian plums were the keepers for pickling. They are delicious fresh, but they are also perfect for jams, pancake syrup, holiday pastry, or spiced and set aside for the winter. This recipe doubles or halves easily for preserving in pint (.5 L) as well as quart (1 L) jars.

YIELD: 4 quart (1 L) jars; or 8 pint (.5 L) jars
SHELF LIFE: Up to 12 months
PROCESSING METHOD: Hot pack; hot-water bath
HEAD SPACE: ½ inch (1.3 cm)
PROCESSING TIME: 15 minutes in a hot-water bath

INGREDIENTS

5½–6 pounds (2.5–2.7 kg) Italian plums with the stems removed

1 teaspoon whole cloves

4 slices ginger, each sliced ⅛ inch (.3 cm) thick and peeled

2½ cups (500 g) granulated sugar

1 cup (145 g) light brown sugar, loosely packed

½ cup (120 mL) fresh orange juice

3 cups (720 mL) white balsamic vinegar

2 cups (480 mL) water

METHOD

Rinse and drain the plums. Prick each of them two to three times with the tip of a sharp knife. (This will prevent them from bursting.) Place the plums in a large, shallow bowl and set aside.

In a medium saucepan, blend all of the other ingredients and bring them to a boil. Reduce the heat and simmer the liquid for another 10 minutes. Remove the pan from the heat, and set aside to cool for 20 to 30 minutes.

Using a strainer, pour the liquid over the plums in the bowl. Cover the bowl with a towel, and allow the plums to set for approximately 8 hours, or overnight.

The next day, use a slotted spoon to lift the plums out of the syrup, and set aside. Pour the liquid into a large saucepan or stock pot. Bring the liquid to a low boil and add the plums. Allow the mixture to cook over medium heat for another 15 minutes, or until the liquid begins to bubble.

Carefully spoon the plums into hot, sterilized jars. Ladle the syrup into the jars, leaving ½ inch (1.3 cm) of head room. Use a bubble freer to release any additional air, apply the lids,

adjust the caps, and process in a hot-water bath for 15 minutes. Remove the jars, and set aside to cool in a draft-free area before storing. Allow the plums to cure for 3 weeks before serving.

YIELD: 6 pint (.5 L) jars
SHELF LIFE: Up to 6 months
PROCESSING METHOD: Cold pack; hot-water bath
HEAD SPACE: ½ inch (1.3 cm)
PROCESSING TIME: 15 minutes in a hot-water bath

INGREDIENTS

2 pounds (896 g) ripe, firm black or purple figs

2 pounds (896 g) ripe, firm, small apricots, each approximately 1–1¼ inches (2.5–3 cm) in diameter

5 cups (1 kg) granulated sugar

2 quarts (1.9 L) water

3 cups (720 mL) white wine vinegar

2 smooth-skinned lemons, cut into slices, each ⅛ inch (.3 cm) thick with seeds removed

1 tablespoon blanched almond pieces per jar

METHOD

Bring 2 quarts (1.9 L) of water to a low boil while you clean the figs. Remove any stem tips from the figs, rinse them, and place them in a shallow bowl. Pour the boiling water over the figs, and allow them to stand until cool. Drain off the water, and set the bowl of figs aside.

Rinse the apricots, and blanch in boiling water for 5 minutes. Transfer them to a basin of cold water, and allow them to sit for 5 minutes. Use your thumbs and fingers to slip the skin away from the flesh, and place them in a colander to drain.

In a medium saucepan, combine the sugar, water, and vinegar. Bring the ingredients to a boil, reduce the heat, and simmer for 5 minutes. Spoon the almonds into each jar. Loosely pack the apricots and figs in layers, adding lemon slices to taste. Pour the hot liquid into the jars, leaving ½ inch (1.3 cm) of head room. Release any excess air with a bubble freer. Apply the lids, adjust the caps, and process for 15 minutes in a hot-water bath. Remove the jars and set aside to cool in a draft-free area before storing.

APRICOTS, FIGS, AND ALMONDS

A plate of apricots, figs, and almonds frequently offers the finale to our favorite Middle Eastern suppers. The trio of tangy, sweet, and nutty flavors offset the intensity of spicy cuisine. While figs and apricots are most delicious when eaten fresh, this recipe carries their "moment of greatness" long after the harvest is over.

PEACHES SUPREME

Add the cast of a summer sunset to your table, and a refreshing aftermath to dinner, with peaches supreme. This recipe blends fresh peaches with crushed raspberries and a touch of nutmeg. While the process does take a little more time than most pickles, the results are well worth the effort. As an option, place one peach seed at the bottom of each jar before packing. The flavor will be memorable.

YIELD: 2 quart (1 L) jars
SHELF LIFE: 6 months
PROCESSING METHOD: Hot pack;
 hot-water bath
HEAD SPACE: 1/2 inch (1.3 cm)
PROCESSING TIME: 25 minutes

INGREDIENTS

 12–14 peaches (any good canning variety)
 1 cup (224 g) fresh raspberries, crushed
 1 1/2 cups (300 g) sugar
 1 cup (240 mL) white wine vinegar
 1/4 teaspoon nutmeg

METHOD

Wash and drain the peaches. Bring 2 quarts (1.9 L) of water to a boil in a large saucepan. Place the peaches in a wire basket, and dip them into the boiling water. Allow the peaches to remain in the pot for 2 minutes. Remove the basket, plunge the peaches into a pan or sink of cold water, then drain. When the peaches are cool enough to handle, slip off the outer skins, cut in half and remove the peach seed. Place the peach halves in a colander, and rinse quickly. Set aside to drain while preparing the pickling solution.

In a medium saucepan, bring the raspberries, sugar, wine vinegar, and nutmeg to a boil. Allow the mixture to bubble for 2 to 3 minutes. Lower the heat while packing the peaches, but remember to keep the liquid very hot.

Gently spoon the peaches into hot sterilized jars (with an optional peach seed). Pour the hot raspberry liquid over the fruit, leaving 1/2 inch (1.3 cm) of headroom. Release the air bubbles. Apply the lids and adjust the caps. Process in a, hot-water bath for 25 minutes. Remove and set aside to cool in a draft-free spot before storing.

ORANGE HOT-PEPPER CATSUP

Every time I share this recipe, I recall my first canning summer in Colorado. I could hardly contain my energy as I waltzed among the tomatoes. We enjoyed a bumper crop in 1978, and I was in tomato heaven. After processing dozens of quart (1 L) jars of sauce, salsa, and whole plum tomatoes, I still needed to use up approximately 25 pounds (11 kg) of tomatoes. I decided to make some catsup. Unfortunately, my enthusiasm allowed me to forget that we probably don't consume more than a pint (.5 L) jar or two of catsup per year. Twenty-five pints of catsup later, a lesson had been learned: Don't make food in quantities that you can't consume!

Fortunately, this recipe makes a manageable amount of catsup, and you can even halve it (or double it) if you like.

NOTE: *This recipe calls for habanero pepper, which measures as one of the hottest chilies on the Scoville scale. Be sure to use rubber gloves when handling this capsicum, or your fingers may get a nasty burn.*

YIELD: 3 pint (.5 L) jars
SHELF LIFE: 12 months or more
PROCESSING METHOD: Hot pack; hot-water bath
HEAD SPACE: ½ inch (1.3 cm)
PROCESSING TIME: 15 minutes in a hot-water bath

INGREDIENTS

4½ pounds (2 kg) firm, ripe plum tomatoes, seeded and halved

1 cup (180 g) onions, chopped

½ cup (90 g) fresh orange pieces

½ cup (120 mL) fresh orange juice

2 jalapeño peppers, stemmed, seeded, and minced

1 habanero chile, stemmed, seeded, and chopped

½ cup (100 g) granulated sugar

½ cup (70 g) light brown sugar, tightly packed

1 tablespoon salt

½ cup (120 mL) white distilled vinegar

METHOD

In a medium saucepan, cook the tomatoes and onions until soft. Set aside to cool for 15 minutes. Transfer to a blender and pulse until smooth. Pour the mixture into a medium saucepan, and set aside.

In the blender, pulse the orange pieces, orange juice, jalapeños, and habanero in the blender. Add this mixture to the tomato-onion blend in the saucepan. Blend in the sugars and salt, and cook over medium heat, stirring constantly or 25 minutes. Add the vinegar and cook until thick.

Pour the hot mixture into hot, sterilized jars, leaving ½ inch (1.3 cm) of head room. Apply the lids, adjust the caps, and process for 10 minutes in a hot-water bath. Remove the jars and set aside to cool in a draft-free area before storing. Allow the catsup to cure for 1 week before serving.

from ke-tsiap to catsup

Today's catsup, a pickled condiment made from vinegar, tomatoes, sugar, and spices, has come a long way from its beginnings as fermented fish brine from China. The original sauce, named *ke-tsiap* in the Amoy dialect, mutated as it traveled around the world. The British kept the fish, often in the form of anchovies or oysters, and added mushrooms, walnuts, and sometimes kidney beans and cucumbers. Using tomatoes from Mexico, American cooks began to develop the sauce that covers countless french fries each year.

cooking with pickled ingredients

MOROCCAN CHICKEN WITH SAFI LEMONS AND OLIVES

Until a few years ago, Moroccan cuisine wasn't very well known outside of Northern Africa. With increasingly efficient transportation, the exotic and, yes, romantic ingredients of faraway kitchens are closer to our doorsteps than ever before. On page 50, you'll find a recipe for preserved lemons. The Safi lemons presented here are similar, but use a complex blend of spices to give them a truly Moroccan flavor. While the assembly and baking of the chicken are easy enough, you'll want to get started in advance curing the lemons, which will take three to four weeks.

SAFI LEMONS

INGREDIENTS

       6 medium lemons
  1 1/3 cups (265 g) salt
       2 cinnamon sticks, each approximately
          2–3 inches (5–7.5 cm) in length
       6 cloves
       8 whole coriander seeds
    5–6 black peppercorns
       2 bay leaves, whole

METHOD

Cut the lemons into quarters, but do not cut into separate wedges. To do this, begin at the top of each lemon and slice to within 1/4 to 1/2 inch (.6 to 1.3 cm) of the bottom of the fruit. Spread each lemon open with your hands, and sprinkle the exposed flesh with a little of the salt. Close the lemons, and place them, one at a time, into a quart (1 L) jar, alternating the lemons with the remaining salt and spices. Gently push the lemons down, squeezing out the juice as you press on the fruit. Lemons cure, or ripen, because of the blend of juice and salt—the spice simply endows the mixture with that touch of the exotic.

You may need to add extra juice if the last lemon isn't completely immersed. Use freshly squeezed, not bottled or processed juice from concentrate. Release any air bubbles, apply the lid, and seal the jar. Allow it to sit in a dark, warm spot in your pantry or kitchen. Turn the jar every day—one day right side up, the next upside down. This allows the salt and the juice to saturate all of the fruit.

When you are ready to use the lemons, simply rinse them under running water to remove any of the natural coating that will cover the surface. Then they are ready to slice, dice, or leave whole in your favorite recipes. Once you've opened your jar, you can keep it in the pantry or the refrigerator, depending on your preference and your climate.

YIELD: 1 quart (1 L) jar

MOROCCAN CHICKEN

INGREDIENTS

  4 1/2–5 pounds (2–2.27 kg) chicken parts,
           rinsed thoroughly and drained
   2 1/2 cups (600 mL) water
   1 1/2 cups (72 g) fresh parsley, chopped
        6 cloves fresh garlic, peeled and sliced
        1 teaspoon sea salt
        1 teaspoon fresh minced ginger
        1 teaspoon ground cinnamon
      1/2 teaspoon freshly ground black pepper
      1/2 stick (60 g) unsalted butter, melted
        4 cinnamon sticks, each approximately
           3 inches (7.5 cm) in length
        3 preserved lemons
        1 cup (224 g) Kalamata olives,
           pitted but whole
      1/4 cup (60 mL) fresh lemon juice
           Lemon zest for garnish

METHOD

Preheat the oven to 350°F (175°C). Place the chicken in a large pot, and add the water, parsley, garlic, salt, ginger, ground cinnamon, pepper, 2 tablespoons of the butter, and the cinnamon sticks. Gently blend the chicken with the water and seasonings until the ingredients are evenly distributed.

Over medium heat, bring the mixture to a boil and cook uncovered for 15 minutes. Remove the pot from the heat, cover, and allow the ingredients to steep for one hour. (Or: Reduce the heat, cover, and allow the ingredients to simmer for 20 to 30 minutes.) Using a large slotted spoon, lift the chicken out of the pot, and place it in an ovenproof baking dish. Set aside.

Heat up the liquid in the pot, and cook, stirring constantly, over medium-high heat until the ingredients begin to thicken. Pour the thickened liquid through a strainer and into a large measuring cup. This will separate any small bones and the larger spices from the sauce. Add the 1/4 cup (60 mL) of lemon juice to this mixture.

Pour the strained sauce over the chicken. Cut the preserved lemons into thick slices and blend them with the olives in a small bowl. Add the mixture to the top of the chicken casserole. Drizzle with the remaining melted butter, and bake, lightly tented with foil, for 15 minutes. Remove the foil and bake, uncovered, for another 10 to 15 minutes. Remove the casserole from the oven, garnish with the lemon zest, and serve immediately.

SERVINGS: 6-8

STIR FRY WITH MING DYNASTY EGGS

In China, poultry has historically been a favorite source of sustenance. Ducks and chickens are easy to raise, and both provide the eggs for what has been affectionately dubbed "thousand-year-old" or "Ming Dynasty" eggs. (See the recipe on page 69.) The ancient method of preserving eggs in salt, lime, and ash, produced a delectable, if somewhat wrinkled, specimen with a creamy yolk and shrunken, slightly green or brown whites. This dish combines the flavor of steeped chicken and braised vegetables with a garnish of the treasured egg. You'll find it's easy to cook and serve direct from the wok.

INGREDIENTS

4 pounds (1.8 kg) chicken, boneless and skinless, cut into small pieces

1/2 cup (120 mL) dark soy sauce

4 tablespoons dry sherry

1 1/2 cups (360 mL) rich strong chicken broth

2 teaspoons sugar

3 tablespoons peanut oil

6 whole scallions, cut into 1-inch (2.5 cm) pieces, green and white parts

2–3 cups (154–224 g) whole baby mushrooms, cleaned and halved

2 cloves garlic, crushed and minced

4 slices fresh ginger root, peeled and minced

1 tablespoon of cornstarch blended with 1/3 cup (80 mL) cold water

4 preserved eggs, cooked and quartered

NOTE: *Serve with sliced bok choy and radishes, drizzled with a little sesame oil and rice wine vinegar.*

METHOD

Rinse the chicken, pat dry with a lint-free cloth, and set aside.

In a small saucepan, combine the soy sauce, sherry, chicken broth, and sugar. Bring the ingredients to a low boil over medium heat, cover, and set aside.

Heat the peanut oil in a wok or heavy skillet and stir fry the chicken over medium-high heat until all sides are golden and slightly crisp. Add the scallions, mushrooms, garlic, and ginger. Stir fry for another 1 to 2 minutes.

Add the hot soy-sherry broth, cover, and simmer for 30 minutes over medium-low heat. Top with the quartered eggs and serve immediately. This dish thickens naturally as it cooks. However, if you prefer a somewhat thicker stir fry, add 1 tablespoon of cornstarch blended with 1/3 (80 mL) cup of cold water to the skillet or wok, allowing the mixture to thicken before adding the eggs.

SERVES: 4–6

GRAVLAX WITH DILL, CAPERS, AND PRESERVED LEMONS

This quickly cured salmon originated in Sweden, and is savored in countries all over the world. Thin, almost transparent slices are traditionally served piled onto slices of pumpernickel. The standard treatment for the fish involves using a whole fillet and allowing it to nestle in salt and sugar for about a week before serving. However, this recipe only requires a day or two for plentiful flavor without an overwhelming cover of saltiness. I serve it with hard-cooked eggs, preserved lemon slices, and fresh light rye. It is also quite wonderful as a side with deep-dish onion quiche. The included recipe for the dill and caper sauce is the perfect complementary condiment.

Be aware that this is a raw-fish presentation. While the cure provides a modicum of preservation for the short-term, it is not comparable to smoke- or chemical-cured salmon products. Use only the freshest fish available, keeping the cured fillet refrigerated before and after serving.

INGREDIENTS

2–2½ pounds (.9–1.1 kg) fresh salmon fillet

2 tablespoons granulated or brown sugar

2 tablespoons kosher salt

2 tablespoons combined white and black peppercorns, crushed

4 ounces (112 g) dill, finely chopped (reserve a few nice sprigs for the garnish

METHOD

Use only fresh salmon! If the fish has a strong odor it is not suitable for gravlax. Rinse the salmon under cool water and pat dry. Place it on a glass plate or nonporous cutting surface. Inspect the fillet for any bones by rubbing your fingers over the surface. Remove bones with tweezers or needle-nose pliers. Combine the brown sugar, salt, and pepper.

NOTE: *You may find that placing the uncovered fillet in the freezer for 15 or 20 minutes will make slicing easier.*

Place fish lengthwise on a flat surface so it is parallel to the countertop. Using a very sharp knife, cut the fillet into thin, horizontal slices from head to tail. Try to keep your slices as close to ⅛ inch thick (.3 cm) as possible—cutting them even thinner would be better. Note that all your slices will not be perfect: the fillet is wider at the head end and all slices will not go the full length.

As you remove the slices, flip each one over and put to the side, arranging each piece to recreate the shape of the original fillet.

For the applying the cure (the sugar-salt-pepper mixture), you will flip and restack the fish back into its original order in a shallow, oblong dish or plate, alternately applying the cure and dill to each slice. To begin, sprinkle a little of the dill onto the dish. Take a slice from the stack of your cut fillet, sprinkle some of the sugar-salt-pepper mixture over it, and gently rub it in on both sides. Then lay the slice on top of the dill. Take the next slice from the stack and apply a generous sprinkling of dill to it, rubbing the dill gently into both sides. Place this slice on top of the slice with cure. Continue alternating each layer, one slice with the cure, one with the dill, until the fillet is back in its original order.

Cover the salmon with plastic wrap, carefully sealing all sides. Place in the refrigerator. Occasionally drain off the juice that seeps out of the fillet. Refrigerate for 24 hours and test for flavor. If you prefer more taste, refrigerate for another 24 hours before serving.

When ready to serve, arrange the gravlax on a platter. To make serving easier, slice down the center of the fillet from head to tail, making sure the knife goes all the way through. Next, slice the fillet crosswise down the entire length to make 1-inch-wide (2.5 cm) rectangles. Garnish the fish with sprigs of fresh dill, thin cucumber slices, and thinly cut slices of the preserved lemon. Serve with the dill and caper sauce. Optional serving companions can be chopped hard-boiled eggs and thin slices of fresh pumpernickel, rye bread, or delicate crackers.

CAPER AND DILL SAUCE

INGREDIENTS

½ cup (120 mL) olive oil

3 tablespoons Dijon mustard

1–2 tablespoons white wine vinegar

2 tablespoons fresh dill, finely chopped

¼ teaspoon each of salt and pepper

1 teaspoon sugar

1 tablespoon capers, roughly chopped

METHOD

Combine all ingredients except the capers, which you add after everything else is well blended. If your mustard is very thick, you may need to thin it slightly with more vinegar.

SERVINGS: 9–12, depending upon the occasion and the guests

CHEESE ENCHILADAS WITH PINEAPPLE SALSA

The enchilada is really a transformed tortilla. The yellow-corn variety, first pounded by hand more than 500 years ago, led to blue- and white-corn tortillas. More recently, those made from flour add culinary diversity. The enchilada can either be dipped in sauce, then filled, and rolled, or dipped in sauce, then fried and filled. The process does tend to be a bit messy, but the result, divine. Regardless of the preparation involved, these succulent, filled creations should always be served fresh and hot. Olé!

INGREDIENTS FOR THE FILLING

- 6 corn or flour tortillas, each 6 inches (15 cm) in diameter
- 2 tablespoons safflower oil
- 1 cup (180 g) sweet onion, chopped
- ½ cup (90 g) pineapple, fresh or canned, well-drained and chopped
- ½ cup (120 mL) pineapple salsa (see recipe on page 000)
- 3 cups (336 g) shredded Monterey Jack cheese
- 1 cup (224 g) sour cream
- ⅛ teaspoon ground cinnamon
- ½ teaspoon salt
- 1 tablespoon safflower oil for baking

NOTE: *These enchiladas are a festive treat when served with sliced mango, avocado, and honeydew.*

INGREDIENTS FOR THE SAUCE

- 8 roasted poblano chilies, peeled and seeded
- 4 roasted yellow bell peppers, peeled and seeded
- 4 roasted plum tomatoes, seeded and coarsely chopped
- 2 jalapeño chilies, seeded and coarsely chopped
- 1 cup (240 mL) chicken broth
- 1 teaspoon salt
- ½ teaspoon ground red or green chili
- ½ scallion, chopped
- ¼ teaspoon ground cinnamon
- 2 tablespoons fresh lime juice

NOTE: *The sauce can be made a day or two in advance, then warmed up for final assembly.*

METHOD

For the sauce, preheat the oven to 500°F (260°C). Place the peppers and tomatoes on a cookie sheet and roast for 20 to 30 minutes, or until the skins swell and begin to turn toasty brown. Remove the cookie sheet form the oven, and use a pair of tongs to lift the peppers into a paper or plastic bag. Seal the bag with a twist tie and set aside for 20 minutes. Allow the tomatoes to cool on the cookie sheet before handling.

When you are ready to blend the sauce, remove the peppers from the bag, peel them, and remove the stems and seeds. Place the peppers and tomatoes into a blender or food processor. Pulse for 3 to 5 seconds or until the mixture is fairly smooth.

In a medium saucepan, blend the jalapeños, chicken broth, salt, chili powder, scallion, cinnamon, and lime juice with a whisk. Add the pepper-tomato mixture, and blend thoroughly into the other ingredients. Bring the sauce to a boil over medium heat and cook for 5 minutes, stirring constantly. Reduce the heat and allow the sauce to simmer for 20 minutes. Remove from the heat and set aside.

For the filling, sauté the onion in the safflower oil in a medium skillet over medium heat until the onion is transparent. Remove the skillet from the heat. Add the chopped pineapple, the salsa, Monterey Jack cheese, sour cream, cinnamon and salt. Blend the mixture with a slotted spoon and set aside.

For the final assembly, begin by heating the oven to 375°F (190°C). Place the pan of sauce over low heat until warm. Ladle ½ to ¾ cup (120 to 180 mL) of the sauce onto the bottom of a shallow 9 x 12-inch (22.5 x 30 cm) baking dish.

On your work surface, have a large dinner plate and a pair of tongs at hand. Using the tongs, dip each tortilla into the sauce in the saucepan, then transfer the tortilla to the plate. Spoon approximately ⅓ cup (80 g) of the filling onto the tortilla and roll it up. As you roll each filled tortilla, place them seam-side down into the baking dish.

Use a pastry brush to apply a light coat of oil to the top of each enchilada. Bake for 20 to 25 minutes, or until the filling begins to bubble. Remove the baking dish from the oven. Transfer the enchiladas to individual plates, ladle additional sauce onto each, and serve hot.

SERVINGS: 6

FUSILLI WITH GOLDEN PASTA SAUCE

The golden hues of the roasted yellow bell peppers in the sauce saturate the fusilli, making this dish glow like a field of ripe wheat at twilight. The sauce (see page 48) can be made several days in advance and refrigerated until you are ready to cook. Serve this dish for dinner with mixed greens tossed with olives and orange sections. You'll find that you can have a delicious and beautiful meal on the table in less than 20 minutes.

When cooked, fusilli winds around itself in long sinuous threads. However, it doesn't really bend or wrap itself easily around your fork, making eating it a bit of an acquired technique. This thick sauce also marries well with weightier pasta, such as fettuccine, penne regatta, or tagliatelle.

INGREDIENTS

2 cups (480 mL) golden pasta sauce (see recipe on page 48)
16 ounces (448 g) fusilli

METHOD

In a medium saucepan, heat the golden pasta sauce over low heat for 10 minutes. Cover and keep warm.

In a large pot, bring 6 quarts (5.7 L) of water to a boil. Stir in one rounded tablespoon of salt. Add the fusilli and cook for 15 to 20 minutes, stirring occasionally, until al dente. Pour the pasta into a colander, then transfer it to a heated bowl.

Add the golden pasta sauce and toss until the fusilli is evenly coated. Serve immediately.

SERVES: 4–6

STUFFED GRAPE LEAVES WITH TOMATO SALAD

I spent my early childhood playing in the shade of our grape arbor. Whenever I examined the grapes for ripeness, I couldn't help but notice the spiny, pointed tips of the leaves—they looked like big, outstretched hands. Upon many of those hands (to my eyes) rested our grapes, rocked and balanced to perfection. As an adult, I encountered those "hands" in a different way, as the grape leaves wrapped themselves around rice and golden raisins during my initiation to the methods of Greek cooking. If you haven't tried making a stuffed grape leaf, at least try eating one—food and hands make good companions.

STUFFED GRAPE LEAVES

INGREDIENTS

16 ounces (453 g) brined grape leaves

1 tablespoon extra virgin olive oil

1 medium sweet onion, diced

1 cup (224 g) long-grain rice

¾ cup (112 g) golden raisins

2–2¼ cups (480–540 mL) water

½ cup (28 g) fresh parsley, finely cut

½ teaspoon salt

¼ teaspoon black pepper

½ teaspoon cinnamon

3 tablespoons fresh lemon juice

¼ cup (60 mL) olive oil

Lemon wedges and fresh parsley for garnish (if serving the grape leaves without the salad)

METHOD

Remove the grape leaves from the brine, unfold them carefully, and place them in a colander. Gently rinse the leaves under cold water, and set aside to drain. In a medium saucepan, sauté the onion in the extra virgin olive oil for approximately 5 minutes, or until the onion begins to turn transparent. Add the rice, raisins, parsley, and 1½ cups (360 mL) of the water. Cover and simmer the ingredients for approximately 15 to 20 minutes or until the water is absorbed. Remove the pan from the heat, then add the salt, pepper, and cinnamon, blending them thoroughly into the rice mixture.

Place a grape leaf on a cutting board or work surface with the stem end toward you and the inside of the leaf facing up (the spine of the leaf should be next to the work surface). Place approximately one tablespoon of the rice mixture toward the base of the leaf, then fold the stem end up over it. The filling should be completely covered. Next, fold the sides toward the center, and roll the filled leaf away from you to form a compact little pillow. Work gently; grape leaves are fragile and not always very pliant, making them easy to tear.

Place 6 to 8 grape leaves at the bottom of a medium Dutch oven or saucepan. Lay the stuffed grape leaves on top, seam side down. Add the lemon juice, olive oil, and the remaining water. Cover with an ovenproof plate or dish to keep the stuffed leaves intact while they cook. Then cover the pan, and cook over medium heat until the mixture begins to boil. Allow the stuffed leaves to bubble for 20 to 30 minutes, or until they are very soft when pressed with a spoon. Gently lift the leaves from the pan, and set them aside to cool. Refrigerate for one hour before serving.

SERVINGS: 6–8

TOMATO SALAD

SALAD INGREDIENTS

4–6 cups (300–448 g) mixed greens

1 medium onion, peeled and sliced into thin rings

3 medium tomatoes, cut into wedges

¼ pound (112 g) feta cheese, cut into cubes

½ cup (112 g) Kalamata olives, pitted

DRESSING INGREDIENTS

⅓ cup (80 mL) white wine vinegar

⅓ cup (80 mL) extra virgin olive oil

2 tablespoons fresh lemon juice

1 teaspoon fresh dill

METHOD

Blend all of the salad ingredients in a small bowl, and set aside or refrigerate until ready to use. For the final assembly, arrange the mixed greens, onion rings, tomato wedges, and feta cubes on a large platter. Place the stuffed grape leaves in the center of the platter. Add the olives. Garnish with lemon wedges and parsley.

Drizzle the salad dressing over the ingredients and serve immediately.

NOTE: *Try serving this salad with slices of warm pita bread and extra lemon wedges.*

CHICKEN AND SHRIMP TERIYAKI

Some say the secret is in the sauce, but I think it's in the oven. This combination of savory sauce, chicken, shrimp, and onions will add an Asian flair to supper time. The sauce can be made two to three days in advance, and doubles easily. It also keeps in the refrigerator for up to 10 days. Marry this teriyaki to rice, noodles, or nothing at all. A side of sliced oranges topped with coconut and a squeeze of fresh lime add additional piquancy to this tangy fare.

INGREDIENTS
FOR THE TERIYAKI SAUCE

- 2¼ cups (540 mL) wheat-free tamari sauce
- 2 fresh lemons, sliced
- 4 cloves of fresh garlic, minced
- 1½ cups (360 mL) cool water
- 1½ cups (300 g) sugar
- ½ cup (120 mL) mirin (rice wine vinegar)
- 1½ teaspoons fresh ginger, grated
- 6 tablespoons cornstarch

FOR THE CHICKEN AND SHRIMP

- 2–2½ pounds (.9–1.1 kg) chicken, skinless and boneless dark meat
- 3 medium sweet onions, peeled and sliced
- 1¼ pounds (.55 kg) fresh jumbo shrimp, butterflied with tails intact
- 6 scallions, chopped, both white and green parts
- 2 preserved lemons, seeded and sliced into strips
- Lemon zest (optional)

METHOD

Preheat the oven to 350°F (175°C)

FOR THE SAUCE

In a medium saucepan, use a whisk or slotted spoon to blend the tamari sauce, lemon, garlic, 1 cup (240 mL) of the water, the sugar, mirin, and ginger. Simmer over medium heat until the entire mixture is hot.

Combine the cornstarch and remaining ½ cup (120 mL) of water in a small bowl until well blended. Stir the cornstarch mixture into the seasoned tamari a little at a time, allowing the ingredients to blend together thoroughly. Continue to stir, cooking the sauce for 5 to 7 minutes over medium low heat. The sauce should be dark, smooth, and thick. Remove the saucepan from the heat and set aside. This yields approximately 2½ cups (600 mL) of sauce.

FOR THE CHICKEN AND SHRIMP

Place the chicken and onions in an ovenproof baking dish that is approximately 2 to 3 inches (5 to 7.5 cm) deep. Brush all sides of the chicken with the teriyaki sauce, pour ¼ inch (.6 cm) of water into the dish, and bake uncovered for 35 to 40 minutes.

Place the shrimp and the scallions in a medium bowl. Add enough teriyaki sauce to thoroughly coat the shrimp and scallions. Add this mixture to the chicken dish, topping the dish with the preserved lemons. Bake for another 5 to 10 minutes, or until the shrimp fans out and turns pink.

Remove the dish from the oven, and allow it to sit partially covered for another 5 minutes. Reheat the remaining sauce over low heat. Drizzle a little more of the sauce onto the chicken dish. If preferred, garnish with the lemon zest. Transfer the remaining sauce to a small pitcher, and serve everything immediately.

SERVINGS: 4–6

HAWAIIAN BREAD

Pineapple vinegar, vanilla, and a touch of ginger merge in this yeast bread for a spicy, tangy, and slightly sweet flavor. It makes a good accompaniment to grilled ginger-soy tuna, as well as to vegetables and rice. However, our favorite use of this delightful bread occurs when it's just a bit dry—we use it to make French toast, which we top with sliced bananas and coconut that have been warmed in brown sugar and butter.

INGREDIENTS

- 6 cups (840 g) bread flour
- 1 additional cup (140 g) bread flour for kneading
- ¾ cup (150 g) granulated sugar
- ⅔ cup (56 g) dehydrated potato flakes
- 2 packages granulated yeast
- 1 teaspoon salt
- ½ rounded teaspoon ground ginger
- ½ cup (120 mL) pineapple vinegar (see recipe on page 41)
- ½ cup (90 g) crushed pineapple, drained
- 3 egg whites
- 1 tablespoon vanilla
- ¼ teaspoon cinnamon
- 1 cup (240 mL) whole milk
- ½ cup (120 mL) water
- ½ stick (60 g) unsalted butter

METHOD

In a large mixing bowl, sift together the flour, sugar, dehydrated potato, yeast, salt, and ginger. Set aside. In a blender, pulse the vinegar, pineapple, egg whites, vanilla, and cinnamon at high speed for 3 to 4 seconds, or until the ingredients are just mixed. Set aside.

Heat the milk, water, and butter in a small saucepan over medium-low heat until the butter melts. Add the milk mixture to the dry ingredients, then blend together using a slotted spoon or your hands. Add the pineapple mixture, blending and kneading it into the flour mixture until the liquid is completely absorbed and the dough begins to pull away from the sides of the bowl.

Turn the dough onto a floured surface and knead, adding the additional flour as necessary to keep the dough from sticking to your hands. Continue to knead the dough for another 15 minutes until the surface becomes smooth and elastic.

Brush another bowl with a little vegetable oil or nonstick spray. Place the dough in the bowl, then cover the bowl completely with a large plastic bag. Set aside to rise for 1½ to 2 hours, or until the dough is double in size.

Preheat the oven to 350°F (175°C). Punch down the dough and shape it into rounds or loaves. You can either bake your bread in two loaf pans, or use a baking stone. If you use pans, brush each with a little oil before putting the bread dough into the pans for baking. Bake on the middle rack in the oven for 25 to 30 minutes, or until the top crust turns golden brown and the loaves sound hollow when tapped. Remove the bread from the oven and set aside for 15 minutes, or until it is cool enough to be transferred to a cooling rack.

NOTE: *You can serve this bread at room temperature or freeze it for future use. Just be sure that the loaves are completely cool and tightly wrapped before placing them in your freezer.*

YIELD: 2 large loaves

OLIVE ROSEMARY BREAD

Olives. Olives with herbs, olives with bread, olives with olives. Throughout France, Italy, the Iberian Peninsula, the Middle East, and America, people eat olives for breakfast, lunch, and dinner. This recipe combines the body of a yeast bread with the redolence of rosemary and the tang of green and black brined olives. Savor it with soup, or toast it and serve it with freshly sliced tomatoes.

INGREDIENTS

- 1 package dry active yeast (approximately 2½ teaspoons)
- 2 tablespoons sugar
- 1 teaspoon salt
- 4 cups (560 g) unbleached bread flour
- ½ cup (120 mL) warm tap water
- 2 large eggs
- 1 stick (115 g) cold butter, chipped
- ¼ cup (56 g) pitted green Cerignola or Spanish olives
- ¼ cup (56 g) Kalamata olives, pitted and chopped
- 1 teaspoon fresh thyme, finely cut
- 2 tablespoons fresh rosemary, finely cut
- 1 egg yolk, beaten with 2 tablespoons warm water

METHOD

Combine the yeast, sugar, salt, and 1 cup (140 g) of the flour in a large bowl until all of the ingredients are blended. Pour in the warm water, blending it into the flour mixture with a fork. Blend in the eggs until they are completely absorbed. Add the butter, and work it into the mixture with your fingers. Be sure to blend the butter into the yeast and flour thoroughly. Add 2½ cups (350 g) of the flour, and knead it in.

Combine the olives, thyme, and rosemary in a small bowl, then add them to the dough. Knead the dough for 7 to 10 minutes, or until it's silky and pliant. Add a little more flour from the remaining ½ cup (70 g) of flour if the dough is a bit sticky. Continue to work the dough until it begins to pull away from the sides of the bowl.

Turn the dough onto a floured surface and continue to knead for another 5 minutes. Place the olive dough into a lightly oiled bowl, turning the dough so that all sides get covered with the oil. Slip the bowl into a large plastic bag, and set aside in a warm, draft-free spot for 1½ hours. When the time is up, the dough should be doubled in size, and ready to bake.

Preheat the oven to 375°F (190°C). Punch the dough down, remove it from the bowl, and form an oblong or round loaf (your choice). Transfer the dough to a baking stone, and brush all sides with the egg-water wash. Bake 25 to 30 minutes, or until the bread is golden brown, firm to touch, and moves easily on the stone.

Remove the bread from the oven, and set aside for 10 minutes. Transfer the bread to a wire rack to cool. Serve warm, or at room temperature.

NOTE: *This bread is especially good with fresh white mozzarella!*

YIELD: 1 loaf

sauerkraut

Although largely associated with German cuisine, sauerkraut helped build the great Wall of China. Over 2000 year ago, workers consumed shredded cabbage fermented in rice wine as part of their daily fare. We're not sure of the exact date of adoption, but sour cabbage eventually made its way to Western Europe, where it became a hit with the Alsatians and the Germans.

OLD-FASHIONED SAUERKRAUT WITH APPLES AND PORK

When August Luchow opened his first restaurant in New York in 1882, it won critical acclaim as well as the attention of people prominent in politics, arts, and social graces. The ambience, the excellent service, and the cuisine continued to satisfy and delight guests for more than seven decades. I first had the opportunity to dine at Luchows in the 1970s, and tasted the best of traditional sauerkraut with apples. This recipe is an adaptation of a dinner savored years ago, and offers a real homemade dimension with freshly brined kraut in addition to white wine vinegar.

INGREDIENTS

6–8 fresh bratwurst or smoked pork chops, depending on the appetites of your guests

2 quarts (2 L) freshly rinsed and drained sauerkraut

1 cup (180 g) coarsely chopped yellow onion

½ stick (60 g) butter

4 large Jonathan apples

½ cup (120 mL) white wine vinegar

1½ cups (360 mL) white wine, or sauterne

1 cup (240 mL) chicken broth or bouillon

½ cup (70 g) brown sugar

2 tablespoons whole caraway seed

NOTE: *This dish marries well with sides of steamed parsnips, redskin potatoes, or carrots with whole green beans.*

METHOD

Heat the oven to 350°F (175°C). In a medium skillet, brown the bratwurst or pork chops over medium-low heat for approximately 10 to 15 minutes, or until all sides are slightly golden brown. Remove the skillet from the heat, and cover. Put the sauerkraut in a colander, rinse, and allow to drain while preparing the other ingredients.

In a Dutch oven, or deep oven-ready pan, sauté the onion in the butter until golden. Add the sauerkraut and cook uncovered, stirring occasionally, for 15 minutes. Remove from the heat.

Wash, core, and cut the apples, and add them to the sauerkraut. Add the white wine vinegar, the white wine, stock, brown sugar, and caraway seed. Blend all of the ingredients with a large slotted spoon and bake, covered, for 30 minutes. Add the pork, cover, and bake for another 15 to 20 minutes. Remove the casserole from the oven, and allow it to sit for 5 minutes before serving.

SERVINGS: 4–6

HOMEMADE MASCARPONE CREPES
CROWNED WITH BALSAMIC STRAWBERRIES

The combination of fresh fruit and dessert cheese remains a classic final touch for dinner or lunch. Add a golden brown crepe, and you offer a truly elegant yet surprisingly simple-to-assemble dessert for your guests. While the entire recipe involves making mascarpone and marinating strawberries in balsamic vinegar, these ingredients can be made a day in advance. And, of course, you can save time by purchasing, rather than making the cheese. However, if you've never made cheese before, mascarpone is an easy introduction—you'll find that homemade is well worth the effort.

MASCARPONE

EQUIPMENT

1 dairy thermometer

1 medium colander

1 large bowl for collecting whey

1 large square of fine cheesecloth

INGREDIENTS

2 quarts (2 L) light cream or half-and-half, preferably organic

½ rounded teaspoon tartaric acid

1 teaspoon fresh lemon zest

½ cup (43 g) almonds, toasted and chopped

METHOD

Heat the cream in a double boiler over medium-low heat. Use the dairy thermometer to monitor the cream's temperature. When the cream reaches 170°F (78°C), lower the heat to barely maintain the temperature. Add the tartaric acid and gently blend it into the cream with a wire whisk. The cream should thicken immediately. If it doesn't, add a bare pinch of additional tartaric acid, blend and keep warm for another 5 to 7 minutes.

Drain the curds. Place a medium colander over a bowl to catch the whey. Line the colander with the cheesecloth, allowing excess material to drape over the sides for covering the curds. Ladle the mascarpone curds into the colander, and bring the excess cheesecloth up over the top, covering the surface of the curds.

Allow the curds to drain for 15 minutes. Lift the colander out of the bowl and pour off any of the collected whey. Place the colander back into the bowl, and transfer to the refrigerator. Allow the covered curds to drain overnight, or for approximately 12 to 15 hours.

Remove the mascarpone from the refrigerator and transfer to a bowl with an airtight lid. Add the lemon zest and the almonds, and gently blend all of the ingredients. Cover and refrigerate until ready to use.

YIELD: Approximately 3 cups (672 g)

BALSAMIC STRAWBERRIES

INGREDIENTS

2½ pounds (1.12 kg) strawberries, fresh, cleaned, and sliced; you may want to reserve a whole strawberry to crown each filled crepe

½ teaspoon salt

¼ teaspoon finely ground black pepper

⅓ cup (67 g) fine, white sugar

1 cup (240 mL) balsamic vinegar, imported and aged

METHOD

Place the berries in a medium bowl. Add the salt, pepper, and sugar. Toss gently to blend with the strawberries, and set aside for 15 minutes. Add the balsamic vinegar. Cover and refrigerate until ready to use.

NOTE: *On page 91 you'll find a recipe for processing whole balsamic strawberries.*

CREPES

Making the crepes and the final assembly comprise the parts of this portion of the recipe. Since organization is the key to success here, a few simple steps will allow you to easily make a batch of crepes. You'll need a nonstick skillet or crepe pan, a soft spatula, a cooling rack, as well as a few sheets of wax paper for stacking the crepes after they cool. I've found it's easiest to first make the crepe batter, then take the strawberries out of the refrigerator, toss them, and let them stand until I am ready to serve.

INGREDIENTS

  2 eggs, extra large

  1 cup (240 mL) milk; you may need a little more

¾–1 cup (84 to 119 g) all-purpose flour

  ⅛ teaspoon salt

  ⅓ cup (75 g) unsalted butter

2–3 tablespoons additional unsalted butter for cooking the crepes

METHOD

In a blender, pulse the eggs and the milk for 3 to 5 seconds. Add the flour and the salt, and pulse at high speed until all of the ingredients blend to form a smooth batter. Pour the batter through a strainer over a large measuring cup, and discard any lumps. Allow the batter to sit at room temperature for 20 minutes. (At this point, take the strawberries out of the refrigerator.)

Melt the ⅓ cup (75 g) of butter in a small saucepan, remove it from the heat, and allow it to cool for a minute or two. Blend the melted butter into the crepe batter with a whisk. The batter should be the consistency of heavy cream. If it's thicker than you like it, blend in a little more milk.

In the skillet or crepe pan, melt approximately 1 tablespoon of the additional butter until it begins to turn a little brown. Pour in ¼ to ⅓ cup (60 to 80 mL) of the crepe batter, and swirl the pan so that the batter completely covers the bottom and a little of the sides.

Cook for 1 to 2 minutes, or until the center of the crepe is set and the underside is turning golden brown. Either jerk the pan, or use a narrow spatula to flip the crepe. Allow it to cook for another minute or two, until the reverse side turns golden brown. Turn the crepe onto the cooling rack. Use the remaining butter and crepe batter to make the rest of the crepes, transferring your cooked crepes to the cooling rack when done. Once the crepes are cool enough to handle, stack them between layers of wax paper.

For the final assembly, remove the mascarpone from the refrigerator and allow it to sit for a few minutes, gently stirring it with a spoon. The mascarpone should be soft enough to easily spread with a spatula or icing knife. Place a spoonful or two of mascarpone in the center of a crepe, and spread it to cover approximately three-quarters of the surface of the crepe. Fold the crepe in half, then in half again, forming a layered triangle. Spoon the balsamic strawberries over the crepe, and crown with a whole berry to serve.

OPTION: *Strain the juice from the strawberries and warm over low heat. Top the crepe with the strawberries, and ladle the warm balsamic juice over the top before crowning with a whole berry.*

YIELD: 12 crepes. Serves 6–12

GRILLED TUNA IN MAUI MARINADE

Maui marinade graces meat, poultry, vegetables, and fruit with ease. I've basted fish, meat, pineapple, and even small cobs of corn for a mixed grill that easily serves six to eight guests. The recipe for the marinade (see page 46) can be made for immediate use or processed for the pantry. We enjoy this recipe accompanied by steamed rice and fresh melon.

FOR THE GRILL

INGREDIENTS

6–8 fresh yellowfin tuna fillets

6–8 slices fresh pineapple, with the skin

Freshly squeezed lime juice to taste

METHOD

Place the tuna and the pineapple in a shallow baking dish and cover both with 1 cup (240 mL) of Maui marinade. Transfer both to a grilling accessory that is suitable for grilling fish, and grill over medium-high heat for approximately 8 minutes. Squeeze fresh lime juice over the grilled fish and pineapple. Serve hot.

SERVINGS: 6–8

MAUI MARINADE

Here's a halved recipes of the marinade from page 46. This is a handy reference if you wish to make it for immediate use. When preparing it for the pantry, see the recipe on page 46 for the processing method and time.

INGREDIENTS

$\frac{1}{4}$ cup (60 mL) white wine vinegar

$\frac{1}{4}$ cup (60 mL) white distilled vinegar

$\frac{1}{2}$ cup (120 mL) soy sauce

$\frac{1}{4}$ teaspoon fine black pepper

$\frac{1}{4}$ cup (85 g) light corn oil

3 tablespoons light brown sugar

2 cloves fresh garlic, peeled and minced

2 tablespoons ginger, peeled and minced

2 small serrano peppers, seeded, stemmed, and minced

Zest of one lime

METHOD

In a small saucepan, blend all of the ingredients with a whisk. Bring the mixture to a low boil over medium heat, and allow it to bubble for 5 minutes. Cool to room temperature for immediate use.

**DESIGNS BY
TRACI TAYLOR**

Jars of homemade pickles make wonderful gifts. You can share the best tastes of a season with family and friends through-out the year. When they open a refreshing jar of tiered oranges, lemons, and kumquats in July, or peaches supereme in February, know that your gifts will be appreciated. Whether you give a jar of preserved lemons to a creative cook or a jar of crispy dills to a favorite uncle, you are giving from your hearth and heart.

You can find a variety of decorative jars from different manufacturers, perfect for putting up a special give-away batch. As an extra bonus, and to share the fun of pickling, enclose the recipe with your gift. So wrap up the classic sweets, pack the hot salsa, and present the spiced pears—following are a few gift-wrap and presentation ideas for your pickles.

NATURALS

Use natural materials when wrapping your pickles. A plain brown bag gets festive with a colorful tie of chili peppers strung on twine or raffia.

Roll corrugated cardboard around a bottle, secure it with raffia, then dress it up with dried or fresh flowers.

Fill a small clay flower pot half full with decorative packing, place the jar in the pot, then tie the two together with string, ribbon, or raffia.

JUST FOR FUN

Take a painted tin and glue half-round plastic beads on the lid, then create a decorative tie using ribbon in a coordinating color. The beads used here are approximately 3/4 inch (1.9 cm) in diameter and have a frosted finish. Before placing the jars in the tin, use a colorful tissue paper as a filler. For a different look use decorative buttons, wood beads, or charms.

BASKETS

Baskets are always in style as the perfect presentation when giving food gifts. Start with a plain basket, then let you creativity take over. The basic ground rule for creating a basket is to nestle your items in the perfect setting of filling material, such as tissue paper, decorative fillings, even potpourri.

The handled basket takes on harvest theme with silk flowers in fall colors. Clip the stems to approximately 1½ to 2 inches (3.8 to 5 cm), then work the stems into the spaces in the basket's rim. Finish with a coordinating ribbon or bow.

You can also place a jar in a basket and wrap both with a beautiful ribbon. The one shown here use colorful potpourri as a filling material. For wrapping the basket and jar, you may find it helpful to use wired ribbon.

HOLIDAYS

Try a gift within a gift. Pack a pint (.5 L) jar into a wooden recipe box, then tie the box with a red-gingham, wired ribbon. Once the jar is removed, the box will come in handy to store a collection of favorite pickle recipes.

Decorate bags with miniature garlands, stick-on stars, glitter, or tinsel—be creative! Involve the kids in fashioning the wrapping during a holiday-time family night. Use colored tissue as an extra filler, insert a jar, and you have a perfect gift.

glossary

ACETIC ACID A colorless, pungent liquid that forms when common airborne bacteria interact with the alcohol present in fermenting solutions, such as wine, cider, or beer. Acetic acid is the core constituent that makes vinegar sour. The Italian term aceto means vinegar.

ACIDIFY To treat with acids or vinegar in order to increase the acid level in foods.

ASCORBIC ACID White crystallized vitamin C. The use of this acid prevents discoloration of fruits and some cheeses.

BOTULISM The poison which is produced by the growth of Clostridium botulinum spores, which thrive in low-acid foods. Such bacteria cannot exist in air, and usually don't grow in high-acid foods. Processing or boiling food destroys these bacteria, and any potential toxin.

BRINE A solution of strong salt water used for pickling. Pickling brine can also contain herbs and spices.

BRINING Processing food in a solution of strong salt water.

CANNER A type of canning equipment for processing jarred food for long-term storage. A canner can be a large pot for hot-water bath processing, or a large pressure canner with dials and instruments for processing low-acid foods. For pickling, you will only need equipment for processing in a hot-water bath.

CITRIC ACID The acid present in citrus fruits such as limes, lemons and grapefruit. Citric acid is an antioxidant and helpful for controlling the color of fruit.

COLD PACK Sometimes called raw pack, the process of filling jars with uncooked, as opposed to heated, food for canning.

FERMENTATION A process which encourages a chemical change in food because of the growth of enzymes or yeast. Fermentation usually causes a change in food flavor, body, and color.

HEADSPACE Also called headroom, is the distance between the food and the top of the jar in which it is stored. Headspace is critical to the pickling or canning process because it allows hot food to expand during processing without breaking the seal that insures preservation.

HOT PACK Filling jars with hot cooked food in preparation for processing.

KOSHER FOOD Food that conforms to Jewish biblical law which dictates what types of food or food combinations may be consumed. Kosher comes from kasher, which in Hebrew means "proper" or "pure."

MOTHER The bacterial slime which causes fermentation in wine, cider, or raw fruit juice, turning them to vinegar. Once a liquid becomes vinegar, the mother can be transferred to another solution as a starter or discarded.

MUST The freshly pressed juice (including any pulp, skins, and seeds) from apples and other fruits. The creation of must precedes fermentation in the vinegar- or wine-making process.

PH BALANCE The ratio of acid to alkaline. In pickling and preserving, foods are separated into high- and low-acid categories. The pH values signal the processing techniques you need to use.

PICKLE The process of preserving food that includes the use of a solution of seasoned brine or vinegar.

PICKLING SALT A fine-grained salt that is used to make brines for pickling. Pickling salt contains no additives, which can frequently create cloudy solutions when pickling. Like most commercially available salt, pickling salt comes from dried lake regions throughout the world.

SEA SALT Salt harvested from ocean water instead of lake-water residue. When using sea salt for pickling, select white grains, as opposed to gray or pale-green. The color indicates the presence of seaweed or other compounds which may cause spoilage.

SAUERKRAUT The fermented mixture of shredded cabbage, spices, and salt.

SEDIMENT The grainy deposit that sometimes rests at the bottom of a bottle of wine.

SHELF LIFE The reasonable amount of time estimated for storing processed food. Eating food within its shelf life, whether processed for the pantry or refrigerator, will ensure consuming goods that are fresh and flavorful.

VACUUM SEAL This is the absence of normal atmospheric pressure in sealed jars which have been filled with a mixture, heated, then allowed to cool to room temperature. As heated food expands, then contracts as it cools in a canning jar, a partial vacuum forms that creates pressure on the jar lid, forcing a seal around the rim.

VENTING The process of forcing air to escape from a jar, either from heat or pressure canning.

VINEGAR A weak solution of acetic acid that forms from the fermentation of wine, cider, beer, or fruit

WATER BATH The process of heating capped, food-filled jars in water in order to dispel the growth of harmful bacteria and promote a vacuum seal. Processing in hot-water baths and pressure canners ensure freshness (shelf life) for long-term storage of preserved foods.

YEAST Fungi which promote fermentation in food. Yeasts grow from common airborne spores and are killed easily when food is processed at temperatures from 140 to 190°F (60–88°C)

bibliography

Alley, Lynn. *Lost Arts*. Berkeley: Ten Speed, 1995.

Bertolli, Paul. "Make Your Own Aromatic, Full-Bodied Vinegar." *Fine Cooking*, October, 1995.

Brissenden, Rosemary. *Asia's Undiscovered Cuisine*. New York: Pantheon, 1970.

Chioffi, Nancy and Gretchen Mead. *Keeping the Harvest*. Pownel, Vt.: Storey, 1991.

Choy, Sam. *Sam Choy's Island Flavors*. New York: Hyperion, 1999.

Ciletti, Barbara. *The Onion Harvest Cookbook*. Newtown, Conn.: Taunton, 1998.

Ciletti, Barbara. *The Pepper Harvest Cookbook*. Newtown, Conn.: Taunton, 1997.

DeWitt, Dave and Nancy Gerlach. *The Whole Chile Pepper Book*. Boston: Little Brown, 1990.

Gordon, Leslie. *The Country Herbal*. New York: Mayflower Books, 1980.

Hupping, Carol. S*tocking Up*. New York: Simon & Schuster, 1986.

Kamman, Madeleine. *The New Making of a Cook*. New York: William Morrow, 1997.

Kasper, Lynne. *The Splendid Table*. New York: William Morrow, 1992.

Kennedy, Diana. *The Cuisines of Mexico*. New York: Harper & Row, 1986.

McCrae, Bobbi A. *The Herb Companion Wishbook*. Loveland, Co.: Interweave, 1992.

Peterson, James. *Fish & Shellfish*. New York: William Morrow, 1996.

Rich, Chris and Lucy Clark Crawford. *The Food Lover's Guide to Canning*. Asheville, NC: Lark Books, 1997.

Rupp, Rebecca. *Blue Corn & Square Tomatoes*. Pownel, Vt.: Storey, 1987.

Sawyer, Helene. *Gourmet Mustards*. Lake Oswego, Ore.: Culinary Arts, Ltd., 1987.

Shepherd, Renne and Fran Raboff. *More Recipes from a Kitchen* :Ten Speed, 1995.

Toussaint-Samat, Maguelonne. *A History of Food*. Malden, Mass.: Blackwell, 1994.

United States Department of Agriculture. *Complete Guide to Home Canning*, 1988

VanGarde, Shirley J., and Margy Woodburn. *Food preservation and safety: Principles and Practice*. Ames, Iowa: Iowa State University Press, 1994.

Williams, Chuck, ed. *Ravioli & Lasagne*. San Francisco: Time-Life Books, 1996.

Ziedrich, Linda. *The Joy of Pickling*. Boston: The Harvard Common Press, 1998.

metric equivalents

DRY MEASUREMENTS

U.S.	Metric
½ ounce	10 grams
1 ounce	14 grams
2 ounces	57 grams
4 ounces (¼ pound)	114 grams
8 ounces (½ pound)	227 grams
16 ounces (1 pound)	464 grams

LIQUID MESUREMENTS

U.S.	Metric
1 teaspoon	5 ml
1 tablespoon (3 teaspoons)	15 ml
2 tablespoons (1 ounce)	30 ml
¼ cup	60 ml
⅓ cup	80 ml
1 cup (8 ounces)	240 ml
2 cups (1 pint)	480 ml
4 cups (1 quart)	1 liter
4 quarts (1 gallon)	3.75 liters

LENGTH

U.S.	Metric
1 inch	2.5 cm

OVEN TEMPERATURES

U.S.	Metric
32°F (water freezes)	0°C
212°F	100°C
300°F (slow oven)	150°C
350°F (moderate oven)	175°C
400°F (hot oven)	205°C

To convert Fahrenheit to Celsius:

subtract 32, multiply by 5, and divide by 9

special thanks...

...to the J. Weck Company for supplying the unusual canning jars featured in this book. You can visit their website at: www.weckhomecanning.com

...to the Beverage People of Santa Rosa, California, (800-544-1867); and Home-Brew Heaven of Everett, Washington, (800-850-2739) for supplies and equipment for making wine, cider, and vinegar—including yeast, oak barrels, pH testers, and mother culture

...and to Traci Taylor of Asheville, North Carolina, thank you for the beautiful gift-wrapping designs.

index